THE
Tuscan
TABLE

JANE NEWDICK AND LYN RUTHERFORD

PHOTOGRAPHY BY SANDRA LANE

EBURY PRESS
LONDON

First published in 1997

1 3 5 7 9 10 8 6 4 2

Text © Jane Newdick 1997
Recipes © Lyn Rutherford 1997; additional recipes by Maxine Clark
Photographs © Sandra Lane 1997

First published in the United Kingdom in 1997 by Ebury Press
Random House, 20 Vauxhall Bridge Road, London SW1V 2SA

Random House Australia (Pty) Limited
20 Alfred Street, Milsons Point, Sydney,
New South Wales 2061, Australia

Random House New Zealand Limited
18 Poland Road, Glenfield, Auckland 10, New Zealand

Random House South Africa (Pty) Limited
Endulini, 5a Jubilee Road, Parktown 2193, South Africa

Random House UK Limited Reg. No. 954009

A CIP catalogue record for this book is available from the British Library.

ISBN 0 09 181420 0

Designed by Alison Shackleton
Photography by Sandra Lane
Styling by Jane Newdick
Food styling by Maxine Clark

Printed and bound in Singapore by Tien Wah Press

THE
Tuscan
TABLE

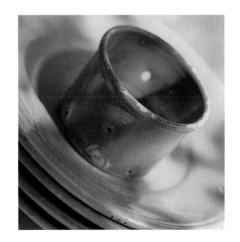

CONTENTS

THE TABLE

Good food is an integral part of Tuscan life. In every household meals are lovingly cooked and served to family and friends, and the experience of eating communally every day is an important one. The food of this region is simple but full of flavour, relying on the freshest seasonal produce cooked in uncomplicated yet delicious ways. The Tuscan table reflects this relaxed attitude to food, using simply made and well-designed glass, china and linen to make the perfect backdrop to every meal, whether it is set in the shade of a vine-covered terrace or the welcoming atmosphere of a country kitchen.

DAPPLED SHADE IS THE SETTING FOR A LAZY
OUTDOOR LUNCH

CHINA

Italy has a long and proud history of producing beautiful and well-designed china. Much of it is exported all over the world, so it is very easy to recreate the authentic look of the Tuscan table. Some pieces are quite elaborate, with hand-painted floral designs, while boldly painted majolica ware is often decorated with mythical or religious scenes. However, even in Tuscany these are used more as special-occasion pieces or to show off in a display than as everyday eating utensils. Colours range from a classic blue on white scroll design to multi-coloured patterns based around fruits and flowers. Reproductions of antique china shapes and painted designs are still made in towns such as Anselmo but are certainly not everyday china. Strong, simple shapes in plain colours or crisp, glossy white are used more commonly in most homes than fussy, patterned versions, and they suit the robust and colourful Tuscan food well. They tend to be functional in style, with good wide edges and deep centres for holding plenty of food. Soup-plate styles or very deep dinner plates with a wide brim are some of the most useful dishes to have as they are very versatile. They are just as suitable for thick bean soups or mixed salads as for stews, polenta, or anything with large amounts of sauce which would not be contained so well by a flat plate. They even double up as dessert or fruit plates, though they are not suitable for most types of antipasti, which are better displayed on smaller, flatter plates. You will probably find that once you have built up a collection of these soup or pasta plates you will use them more than any others in your kitchen. Plain cream or white versions, with or without a decoratively shaped edge, are endlessly useful and can be used to show off every type of food to its best advantage.

Tuscans eat plenty of bread at mealtimes and are likely just to take a piece and place it straight on the table beside their main plate. Or they may put it on

COOL WHITE PASTA OR SOUP PLATES ARE THE BACKBONE OF THE TUSCAN TABLE, TO BE USED FOR MANY DIFFERENT DISHES

the plate with their food, breaking off small pieces as the meal progresses and dipping them into any juices and dressings. Small side plates are a nicety that you don't really need, unless the meal is a more formal affair. Even if this is the case, side plates don't necessarily have to match the main dinner plates.

Day-to-day meals need china that is sturdy enough to withstand rough handling and constant use. Fine porcelain has a place but only for very special occasions, and even then it can seem slightly out of place with the simple, gutsy food of the region. It is better to add a sophisticated note with the use of plain colours and well-designed shapes than worry too much about having the best-quality fine bone china. Salads can easily be served after a main course in the same dish which has been wiped clean with bread. This is all part and parcel of the thrifty but sensible way of going about things in Italy. If you prefer, you can, however, provide slightly smaller deep soup plates or bowls for salad, which might match or contrast with the dinner plates. Mixed salads, though, are nice served on large, flattish plates with the leaves and delicious extra ingredients piled loosely in the middle.

Big china salad bowls are vital in Italy, where salad may be served to several people at a time, and these deep bowls double up as ideal dishes from which to serve pasta. Italians never serve pasta on to plates and then top it with sauce, as is often the case outside Italy. First they warm the bowl, then the piping hot pasta is drained and turned into the bowl, where it is gently but thoroughly mixed with the sauce and served out to everyone. The exact amount of sauce is always carefully calculated and the shape of the pasta is chosen to complement the sauce perfectly. A couple of these large bowls will be invaluable when serving out Tuscan food. Always remember to buy larger ones than you think you will need, as plenty of extra room is vital for tossing the salad properly with its dressing or combining pasta and sauce quickly and efficiently. They can also be used as mixing bowls for cooking, especially for cake or bread making.

THICK TERRACOTTA IS GLAZED IN SUBTLE CREAMS, OCHRES AND BUTTERMILKS

Breakfast is a meal most often eaten on the move in Tuscany. A quick espresso and a delicious sweet and often custardy filled bun is a typical morning habit, taken in a café or bar but rarely at home. You may prefer a more leisurely affair, with fruit or bread and preserves, or a protein-based meal such as eggs or cheese. So plates and bowls may be required and, of course, the essential coffee cup. This can be large enough to hold a frothy cappuccino or small and neat for a shot of the blackest possible espresso. With the rise in popularity of coffee made the Italian way, there are plenty of ranges to choose from. Fine china or chunky earthenware – it all depends how you like to drink your coffee. Often every member of a household has his or her own special preference, and if you have a good assortment of cups all needs and tastes can be catered for.

Small bowls of all shapes, styles and sizes are infinitely useful at the Tuscan table. You will find them invaluable for holding coarse salt, freshly grated Parmesan cheese, olive oil for dipping bread into, olives of all kinds, as well as little delicacies for the antipasti spread. The bowls can be made from china, earthenware or rich terracotta glazed on the inside. They may be perfectly plain or have a single or double handle. You might like to start a collection of different sizes in bright colours to add colourful accents to a plainer table setting, or you could look for authentic Italian splatterware glazes, especially in deep viridian green over white. These look good on small dishes but can be overpowering on larger ones.

Many Tuscan dishes, such as hearty bean soups or meat or vegetable stews, are cooked slowly in the oven or simmered on top of the stove until meltingly soft and tender. These are best served straight to the table from their original cooking dish, so you will need a collection of ovenproof earthenware or something similar. This kind of rustic, earthy dish seems to improve with age, almost

CLOCKWISE FROM TOP LEFT: MODERN VERSIONS OF OLD IDEAS FOR CHINA, WITH A THICK CREAM GLAZE OVER SIMPLE CLAY SHAPES • BLUE SPOTS ADD DASH TO A PLAIN AND SIMPLE COFFEE CUP • TWO TINY BOWLS ENCLOSED BY A WONDERFUL WAVY-EDGED DISH • A SIMPLE AND TIMELESS CREAM JUG FOR FLOWERS, DRINKS OR JUST TO LOOK AT

imparting an extra dimension to the food that's cooked in it. Round, oval, oblong or square, the choice is yours. Obviously, it is easier to cook a whole fish in an oval or oblong dish than a round one, whereas the round one would suit a baked vegetable dish such as courgettes cut into small rounds or aubergine casseroles. Baking dishes do not need to be very deep but a few taller, lidded pots are excellent for bean recipes or for large pieces of meat that need long, slow simmering.

Other types of food need to be transferred to serving dishes before being carried to the table. At informal meals, the grilled foods so beloved of Tuscans can be served straight on to each plate, but for special occasions a large, colourful platter can make a wonderful backdrop for a glistening whole fish, deliciously browned and crisp, still bubbling from the heat of the charcoal and surrounded by grilled baby vegetables. Buy the biggest serving dishes you can as it is better to have too little food on a large plate than too much crammed on to a small one. If you have chosen plain coloured plates to eat off, colourful or decorated serving dishes and bowls are a good way of adding detail and interest to the overall look of the table. While fussy decorated plates can be distracting to eat from, a large platter with a patterned edge can become the main attraction on an otherwise restrained table setting. These can also be your more precious or even oldest pieces, as they won't get such regular wear and tear but just make an appearance every now and again.

Very specialized kinds of china are rare on the Tuscan table, though people may have an old-fashioned formal dinner service that they reserve for special occasions. It is more important to have a wide selection of simply shaped dishes that can double up for many different purposes than to try and find exactly the right dishes for asparagus, for example. Just remember to keep things informal and you won't go far wrong.

CLOCKWISE FROM TOP LEFT: OLD MAJOLICA PLATES IN BEAUTIFUL ITALIAN AQUAS, BROWNS AND GREENS • EARTHY BROWNS COMBINE ELEGANTLY WITH SHARP AQUA BLUE • SUNNY YELLOW PLATES ARE CHUNKY YET SMART • AN OLD BOWL HAS A VIGOROUS YET STRANGELY RESTRAINED DESIGN INSIDE AND OUT

GLASS

Glass plays an important role on the Tuscan table. Generously sized tumblers for everyday meals and suave, stemmed glasses for special occasions are always required for the large quantities of wine that are an integral part of any Italian meal. At large gatherings or family celebrations, a good number of jugs and carafes is needed to hold plenty of drink, whether it be wine, lemonade or water, while smaller, more refined drinking glasses are generally used for special liqueurs or after-dinner drinks. Such a versatile material as glass has been put to many other uses, too, from plates and elaborate cakestands to simple sets of olive oil and vinegar bottles and colourful serving bowls for salads, vegetables and desserts.

In their effortlessly stylish way, the Italians have succeeded in keeping the best of their old traditions alive while embracing all that is good in modern design, as well. Perhaps only in Italy is it possible to enter a tiny, cramped, dark, old-fashioned bar on a scorching hot summer afternoon and to be rewarded with an exquisitely refreshing, perfectly chilled white wine, served in a modern and elegantly designed, long-stemmed glass. As always in this country it is the detail that is significant, and the clever juxtaposition of ancient with new. In Italy this is always achieved with a certain daring and flair, as well as with perfect sensuality.

When choosing drinking glasses for the Tuscan table, remember that scale is important. The food is hearty and generous, the flavours simple but strong, and wine is drunk in the same spirit. Don't choose small, skimpy shapes but go for bold, sturdy ones – generally plain, clear glass although there is a tradition for coloured glass, too. Some people find drinking wine from anything but clear glass strange. However, for everyday quaffing of table wines rather than the finest vintages, coloured tumblers can be fun, and are perfect for informal outdoor meals and picnics.

FOR TRADITIONAL VIN SANTO, A TRADITIONAL GLASS TO DRINK IT FROM

Shapes for drinking glasses vary, though squat, round or faceted tumblers are generally used for wine or soft drinks and water. With so many meals being eaten outside, and often dozens of people sitting down at table to eat, stacking glasses or glass carriers are very useful. The carriers usually have a handle and six or so spaces to hold the tumblers. Glass tumblers are generally inexpensive to buy and designed to withstand quite rough handling. These days, of course, there are lots of variations on the theme, often using recycled glass in a soft greenish colour or stronger shades. Once you start drinking wine from a tumbler you'll be pleasantly surprised to find it makes the whole business more relaxed and homely, as befits family meals and informal lunches and suppers. Classic wine glass shapes seem to be universal but there is a fondness for short-stemmed trumpet-shaped versions with a sensible low centre of gravity and a good large flute to hold the drink. Some of these shapes are reminiscent of glasses made in early Roman times, particularly as the glass is so thick. You can even find jugs made today that have the characteristic Roman-style thin rope of glass encircling the neck or handle, which look like something you might see on an ancient fresco.

Vin Santo is a Tuscan dessert wine drunk at the end of a meal, often instead of dessert. Hard, twice-baked *cantucci* biscuits containing almonds or hazelnuts are dipped into the rich, sweet wine to soften and flavour them. It is an addictive process once you start dipping and drinking. Normally served in small, elegant liqueur glasses, Vin Santo is rather like a sweet sherry or Madeira but with its own very distinctive taste.

Salads can look beautiful served from a deep, roomy glass bowl which displays the vivid green of fresh leaves. Choose plain or bubble glass or even a soft frosted glass for a very elegant and pretty effect. Glass or metal salad servers will complete the picture. Tuscan salads are often dressed at the table and, because the olive oil is of such high quality in this part of Italy, it is usually put on the table in a small bottle along with salt, pepper and vinegar, so everyone

FRESH LEMONADE WAITS IN THE COOL IN A COMFORTINGLY LARGE JUG

can dress their salad the way they like it. In fact the rich, peppery oil is also drizzled over soups, cooked vegetables and other dishes according to each diner's taste. Little sets of two glass bottles are very common, one for oil and one for vinegar, often in a metal carrying rack. A stoppered glass oil bottle is useful in the kitchen, too, for measuring out small amounts of the precious greeny-gold liquid.

Desserts are saved for special celebrations and rarely served at ordinary meals, so there are few glass dishes and pretty serving bowls. Instead, fruit, usually locally grown, is commonly eaten to round off a meal, with ripe pears, figs, peaches, melon or grapes being simply peeled or cut up on a plate by each diner as required.

On a more practical note, plain and simple glass storage jars and containers can be filled with delicious preserves such as roasted and marinated vegetables, olives with herbs and stuffed anchovies. These and other piquant additions to the antipasti spread are suitable to be brought straight to the table. No one would dream of bothering to decant such things into a smarter dish – a jar stood on a plate with a long-handled fork or spoon with which to scoop out the delicacies is all you need. There are many versions of the classic glass preserving jar, some with a screw top and some with a spring-clip lid. Choose whichever suits your needs best but always go for the type with a wide neck so that large items can be packed in easily. These jars are extremely useful for both long- and short-term storage of all kinds of foods; even a few olives bought loose can be kept in a jar, topped up with fresh olive oil and a few sprigs of herbs to give piquancy. On the same theme, herbs or whole spices can be added to glass bottles of oil for cooking; the oil will slowly absorb their flavours and it looks good enough to display in the kitchen as an edible and thrifty decoration.

CLOCKWISE FROM TOP LEFT: LITTLE TUMBLERS ARE THE MOST PRACTICAL FOR OUTDOOR MEALS • A GENEROUSLY SIZED WINEGLASS FOR A GENEROUS CHIANTI • NO TUSCAN TABLE WOULD BE COMPLETE WITHOUT OIL AND VINEGAR BOTTLES FOR THE SALAD COURSE • OLD GLASS JARS AND BOTTLES STILL LOOK AS GOOD TODAY AS THEY EVER DID

LINEN AND CUTLERY

Tuscan cooking is simpler than that of any other part of Italy but soundly based on the use of the finest ingredients. Complementing this food successfully with your table dressing can be achieved on the same principles. Simple fabrics, plain colours, good textures and classic patterns make the very best backdrop for colourful and characterful food.

The people of Florence have long been known as sober and modest in their attitude to food and eating, with a well-documented streak of austerity at the table. Though enjoying good food and plenty of it, they have always preferred simplicity to excess. The Florentines began to observe table manners around the twelfth century – well before the French court, where, as was the custom at the time, people generally ate with their hands. All over Tuscany a tradition of meals as large communal or family affairs has persisted, with people sitting chatting at a long table while eating in a relaxed and leisurely fashion. Even more formal occasions such as a wedding feast are likely to turn into noisy, happy gatherings with the good food and copious wine mellowing the company. However, although people are unlikely to stand on ceremony, at most meals certain standards are observed. If there is a cloth it will be spotlessly laundered, crisp and fresh. Only the minimum amount of cutlery will be provided but it will be clean, sturdy and functional. Large napkins are important for eating such delicious but frequently messy food – think of pasta and sauces, dressed salads and grilled foods which may be eaten with eager fingers.

Even in small country restaurants in Tuscany, standards are very high. At first glance the table may look sparse but there will be everything you need and all of it of good quality. To recreate the look and feel at home, choose things with care. Natural fabrics for cloths and napkins are always the most pleasant to use and they launder well time and time again. Cotton and linen are the

THE ELEGANCE OF A PERFECTLY STARCHED AND ROLLED NAPKIN ON AN EMBROIDERED
CLOTH. COLOUR WOULD SPOIL THE EFFECT

obvious choices, but of course they take a certain amount of work to keep them pressed and looking good. If plain white or cream seems too austere for a tablecloth, choose a rich ochre or neutral sand colour or even a rich deep sienna brown or rust. Accents of a brighter colour can look good, too: try adding turquoise napkins, for example, to a neutral or deep chocolate-coloured linen tablecloth. Coloured fabrics left outdoors on a garden table will fade fast in the summer sun, even in northern climates, so bring them in as soon as the meal is finished unless you prefer the softly sun-faded look which can be really pretty. Plain fabric is smart and simple but neat stripes or checks have a Tuscan feel, too. These can be bold prints or more laid-back self-weave fabrics. Sometimes a more luxurious look is needed for a special dinner or celebration. A subtle damask or even lace cloth over a plain fabric can add just the right amount of detail, plus, of course some big, stiffly starched napkins. For large-scale outdoor eating where you may need to put two or more tables together to seat everyone, use sheets as a base for the table and throw smaller cloths in a patchwork over them. No one will expect a banquet-sized cloth at this kind of occasion.

Not every meal needs a cloth, especially if your table looks good, though napkins are always needed. At outdoor meals for a large crowd it is perfectly acceptable to use the biggest and best-quality paper napkins to save on laundry and extra work. Outdoor meals eaten from garden furniture look inviting with a bright and cheerful cloth spread out. To hold the cloth in place if there are sneaky breezes about, use special clips or attach small weights to each corner of the cloth to secure it. If you frequently eat outdoors in summer you will need a good supply of tablecloths to keep up with meals. Things seem to get spilt more often outdoors, where everyone is more relaxed and less careful.

Cutlery can be as simple as you like. Old or new, matt or shiny, plain steel, silver plate, or with wood, bone or plastic handles – they can all look good. Just

BY KEEPING TO A THEME YOU CAN BUILD A COLLECTION OF LINEN SUITABLE FOR ANY MEAL. HERE IT IS SHADES OF COFFEE, WITH CREAM AND WHITE

choose whichever you prefer, or perhaps invest in a colourful and inexpensive set kept just for outdoor eating. You don't have to have matching sets of everything but it is best to keep to one theme whether it is mismatched but similar old silver plate or bright, plastic-handled cutlery in a range of cheerful colours. Tuscans would probably laugh at us for using a spoon as well as a fork to eat tricky pasta shapes such as spaghetti but most of us don't have the confidence that comes from having eaten the stuff many times a week since we were small children. For most meals a knife, fork and spoon are more than adequate to cope with everything, plus, perhaps, small clean knives for the fruit course. Using fingers is never frowned upon at the times when it makes sense to use them. To save having to lay out masses of cutlery if your meal spreads to several courses, as it can in Tuscany, just ask everyone to hold on to their knives, forks and spoons as each course progresses and plates get cleared away. It's all part of the relaxed, easy atmosphere. If you are taking cutlery outside for an *al fresco* meal, either wrap each set in a napkin and lay the bundles in a shallow basket or on a tray to make carrying easier, or simply put all the cutlery you will need for the meal, handle-end upwards, in a jug or sturdy upright container from which people can help themselves.

Apart from cutlery to use for eating at table, you will also need a good serrated knife for cutting bread, a pair of well-designed salad servers that really work and lots of large spoons and flat spatulas for serving out cold dishes and slices of things such as tarts. Serving spoons can be made of metal but wood has a good feel to it and suits the rustic style of the food. Two-pronged forks are ideal for lifting slices of meat or marinated vegetables from their dish or jar on to the plate. Some other invaluable pieces of cutlery to have at table are a range of small spoons for retrieving olives and other things packed into jars. Look out for spoons with small bowls but extra long handles.

CLOCKWISE FROM TOP LEFT: TURQUOISE-BLUE PLASTIC-HANDLED CUTLERY LOOKS FRESH AND CONTEMPORARY • RICH CHOCOLATE LINEN WITH SUBTLE BLUE STITCHING BENEATH ROUGH, WOODEN-HANDLED SALAD SERVERS • MISMATCH YOUR NAPKINS AT *AL FRESCO* MEALS — NO ONE WILL MIND • BRILLIANT TURQUOISE LINEN BLUER THAN THE MEDITERRANEAN

FLOWERS AND DECORATIONS

In keeping with the mood of the rest of the setting, the flowers on the Tuscan table are likely to be so casual as to appear completely spontaneous and natural. Elaborate arrangements and fussy containers are rarely seen; a bunch of something bright and simple picked from the garden or roadside and stood in a jug or tumbler is far more appropriate. Even if the meal is held outdoors there is still room for flowers. They can complement what is on the table or make a bold, bright contrast to it. A single type of bloom or a riotous mix of colours both look equally good.

Tuscan winters can be quite cold and cheerless, with little to pick in the way of flowers, but a pot or two of something growing or a small posy from the flower shop can brighten the table instead of fresh cut blooms. In spring, summer and autumn there is no shortage of flowers and beautiful natural things to enhance the appearance of the dinner table. The first few small spring flowers, such as violets, deserve to be given pride of place, then, as the season progresses there may be wild poppies and daisies growing amongst the crops to choose from and later a few precious dahlias or rudbeckia from the garden. Italian gardens are rarely full of flowers. They tend towards formality, with plenty of evergreens, clipped hedges and edging, but certain flowers such as roses and lilies are popular. The floral symbol of Florence is the iris, and in parts of Tuscany the pale mauve *Iris fiorentina* is still grown commercially to produce orris root, used in the fragrance industry as a fixative and perfume. Flowers of all kinds are grown in terracotta pots and containers, which are displayed on terraces, down flights of steps or wherever colour is needed near the house. Pelargoniums in vivid clashing pinks, reds and scarlets are abundant. Small stems of these pot-grown plants last well as a cut flower and have the kind of simple charm that is ideally suited to the Tuscan table. If you have plenty of space on

PREVIOUS PAGE: VIVID BLUE LARKSPUR CONTRASTS WITH A CLOUD OF ACID GREEN FENNEL FLOWERS TO DECORATE AN OUTDOOR LUNCH TABLE. OPPOSITE: JAUNTY PEARS, EACH WITH A CURLY STALK, MAKE A CHARMING AND UNUSUAL CENTREPIECE

an outdoor table, you could just put a pot of geraniums straight amongst the dishes. Larger-scale shrubs growing in the garden can be raided all through the year for their glossy leaves and, possibly, scented flowers or berries. Roses look wonderful, whether just a single perfect bloom or a great mass of flowers. Choose loose-petalled, preferably old-fashioned roses, clustered together in a low bowl or basket for a natural garden look. Herbs play an important part on the Tuscan table, so remember to add them to bunches of flowers or use them alone for cool, green, scented posies.

Often taken for granted, ripe fruits in season are usually ravishing to look at. Pile fruits on a stemmed dish or spread them out carefully on a shallow basket, plate or tray. A handful of perfect velvety figs spread out on a fig leaf, or a pile of blushing peaches on a mat of vine leaves, makes a centrepiece to vie with the most glamorous of flowers. In winter lemons and oranges make bold, bright displays, best contrasted with fresh green bay leaves or their own citrus leaves. Some vegetables are pretty enough to display in this way: tiny *zucchini*, or courgettes, with their flowers attached, or miniature squashes, look pretty in a deep bowl, while tomatoes on the vine make colourful decorations. Even a bowl of deep purplish red-skinned onions can look rich and magnificent for a winter table.

Choose containers for flowers and fruits that are sympathetic in style to the rest of the china and glass on the table. Big rustic jugs make excellent holders for tall grasses, cornfield flowers or heavier stems of shrubs. They can be neutral in colour, plain terracotta coloured or brightly glazed and even patterned, depending on the other china you are using. Unsophisticated glassware such as recycled items or coloured glass looks good filled with flowers, while smaller-scale drinking tumblers are suitable for small posies and bouquets of mixed garden flowers.

CLOCKWISE FROM TOP LEFT: AN EXQUISITELY NETTED MELON IS JUST AS DECORATIVE AS A BUNCH OF FLOWERS • POPPIES EDGE THE ROADS IN TUSCANY AND GROW IN DRIFTS THROUGH THE MEADOWS • CLASSIC MARBLE AS OLD AS THE HILLS DISPLAYS FRESH YOUNG ARTICHOKES • RED-SKINNED ONIONS LOOK GLAMOROUS IN A DEEP WOODEN BOWL

BOARDS, BASKETS AND SERVING THINGS

Besides the most obvious requirements of the Tuscan table, such as cutlery, glasses and plates, there are lots of other items that can be very useful to give the right feel. They fall into a category of extras which, while not being vital on their own, help to make the whole thing look finished and authentic. They also tend to be made from materials not dealt with elsewhere in this book, such as wood, basketware and metal. Rustic and often handmade, they add an earthiness and texture that are very sympathetic to the Tuscan style of food.

Wood has always been fairly abundant in northern Italy and used generously for building interiors, furniture, flooring and smaller everyday items. It can be shaped into simple flat slabs for boards or paddles or turned on a lathe to make bowls and deep plates. The thinnest slivers of chestnut wood are commonly used for woven baskets or fruit punnets, while olive wood is turned to make small, densely grained bowls. Long-handled wooden paddles were traditionally used to take bread in and out of wood-fired ovens. The loaves were deftly flicked on or off the paddles by skilled bakers who, as in every country these days, are at risk of becoming a dying breed. Over the years and after countless bakings, these paddles took on great character and developed a fine patina. Short-handled boards or paddles make functional and beautiful surfaces for serving or displaying foods. They are ideal for cheeses or breads, being light to pick up and easy to pass around the table by their handle. Look out for old, well-worn ones or modern versions. Ordinary boards for bread or cheese or for serving antipasti from are useful to have, too, especially if you make a collection of several different sizes to suit every occasion. Small wooden bowls are useful for holding olives, nuts and little savoury bits and pieces. Larger ones are

AN EXQUISITE OLIVE WOOD PLATTER LARGE ENOUGH TO BE A TRAY AND TWO TURNED WOODEN BOWLS

not usually big enough for salads to feed a crowd, so china bowls, which can be made on a grander scale, are generally more popular.

Baskets are, of course, also made from wood but in a rather different form. They make excellent containers for dry foods such as breads, biscuits, nuts and so on. Most rural communities have a tradition of weaving baskets to local designs, sometimes making them for quite specific purposes such as draining fresh cheeses or gathering crops. All kinds of thin, whippy twigs or rushes are used for baskets, with willow and hazel being two of the most popular. Flat baskets lined with leaves make excellent cheese trays, while deeper ones are just right with a napkin inside for holding slices of bread. While fewer and fewer baskets are made locally these days, there are always plenty to choose from that have been imported from other parts of the world and these often look perfectly authentic.

The use of metal as a material for containers and utensils is an ancient tradition. While we might think of it as a purely functional material today, it has a long and honourable history of being manufactured by hand from earliest times in imaginative and highly decorative ways. Pewter, silver, silver-plated copper or brass, gold and steel have all been used to make plates, jugs, goblets and trays. Metal can be engraved and punched, raised and repoussed, though the plainest pieces usually appeal most to modern tastes. Old pieces of pewterware still survive and are affordable but many of the more precious antique metal pieces are too valuable and rare to be used in households. One area of metalwork that still flourishes and has even had a renaissance in the last few years is decorative wirework. Fine wire bent and woven into bowls, trays, baskets and containers has a simple charm to it which blends in very happily with both rustic and sophisticated settings. The Italian versions are often finer than similar French wirework. The finest pieces made today are quite expensive but, treated with care, will last for many years. If you examine some of this fine wirework closely you begin to see how much work is involved, as very often each indi-

ALABASTER, GLASS AND WOOD ALL COMBINE AS SERVING BOWLS FOR ANTIPASTI

vidual strand is tied to every one it crosses. This means that each piece takes hours of delicate, painstaking work to produce. The fine tracery of dark lines forms a beautiful background for anything put on or inside the wire shapes, so it is not surprising that they have become popular again. Like basketware, these lovely wire trays and baskets can be lined with cloths or leaves to make a soft background for easily damaged fruits or delicate cakes and biscuits. When not in use they look very attractive hanging against a plain background.

Tazzas, or stemmed dishes, made from marble, wood, metal, glass or china have a solidity and style that is thoroughly in keeping with the rest of the Tuscan table. Their wonderful timeless feel is reminiscent of ancient statues and columns. Having dishes of different heights on a table is a very useful means of fitting more on, as flatter dishes can sit under the shade, as it were, of the stemmed dishes. They also show off food rather well, turning a group of ordinary fruits into a still life or a plain pudding into a glamorous dessert. When not in use at the table, these dishes are elegant enough to display anywhere in the kitchen or dining room, empty or filled.

If you can find any dishes or *tazzas* that are made from marble or alabaster then these have exactly the right feel to suit the Tuscan table. The soft colours and subtle surface patterns of these very Italian materials make the most beautiful background to many different kinds of food. Generally marble and alabaster used for domestic pieces come in the colour range of buff, pale peachy pink, greys and all shades of cream. While they might seem incredibly impractical for these days of dishwashers and easycare everything, one lovely marble dish will always be the star of the table setting and worth cherishing. Fruits of all kinds look their best displayed on marble and so do little still life arrangements of colourful vegetables in the summer months or nuts and dried fruits during the winter.

CLOCKWISE FROM TOP LEFT: WOODEN BATS FOR TAKING BREAD IN AND OUT OF THE OVEN CAN BE USED FOR SERVING MANY SORTS OF FOOD • AN ELEGANT AND BEAUTIFUL FINELY WOVEN BASKET HOLDS BLUSHING SUMMER PEACHES • ITALIAN WIRE WORK IS COMPLICATED AND BEAUTIFUL • PANFORTE SITS ON A RUSTIC WOVEN TRAY

RECIPES

Tuscan cooking is refreshingly straightforward. There are no rigid rules to follow, no complicated techniques to master, and only a handful of basic ingredients. Sunripened tomatoes, locally grown herbs, vegetables, and fruit, beef from local breeds, game in season and, most important of all, superb olive oil, are all staples of the Tuscan table. The secret is to choose the ingredients with care and prepare them with respect. Recipes in this chapter range from traditional dishes such as **Ribollita** and **Panforte di Siena** to modern classics such as **Red and Yellow Peppers Stuffed with Monkfish**. Remember that in Tuscany no two cooks ever prepare a dish in the same way, so don't be afraid to adjust seasonings to suit your own taste.

SOUPS

PAPPA AL POMODORO (TOMATO, BREAD AND GARLIC SOUP)

A mush or *pappa* of the fruitiest olive oil, country bread and sweet, ripe tomatoes, flavoured with garlic and herbs.

Serves 4

225 G/8 OZ DAY-OLD COARSE COUNTRY BREAD, WITHOUT CRUSTS, SLICED

ABOUT 75 ML/5 TBSP EXTRA VIRGIN OLIVE OIL

3 GARLIC CLOVES, PEELED AND CRUSHED

2 SPRIGS OF FRESH OREGANO

1 SMALL LEEK, WHITE PART ONLY, FINELY CHOPPED

700 G/1½ LB VERY RIPE, SWEET TOMATOES, PREFERABLY PLUM TOMATOES, CHOPPED

1 LITRE/1¾ PINTS/4 CUPS HOT LIGHT CHICKEN STOCK

GOOD HANDFUL OF FRESH BASIL LEAVES, ROUGHLY TORN

SALT AND FRESHLY GROUND BLACK PEPPER

Arrange the bread in a single layer on a baking sheet and place in an oven preheated to 150°C/300°F/Gas Mark 2 for 15–20 minutes, until dried out but not coloured. Tear into pieces and set aside.

Heat 30 ml/2 tbsp of the oil in a large saucepan, add the garlic and cook for a few minutes, until it just begins to colour. Stir in the oregano sprigs and the leek and cook for a minute longer, then add the tomatoes and the bread. Cook, stirring, over a medium heat until the mixture forms a coarse pulp. Gradually add the stock to the pan, stirring the mixture to form a thick, mushy pulp. Add most of the basil and some seasoning and simmer gently for 20 minutes, stirring frequently.

To serve, adjust the seasoning to taste, then pour the soup into 4 serving bowls. Sprinkle each serving with a few torn basil leaves and drizzle with the remaining olive oil.

FLORENTINE RED ONION SOUP

Serves 6

75 ML/5 TBSP OLIVE OIL

1 KG/2¼ LB RED ONIONS, PEELED, HALVED AND
 THINLY SLICED

2 CELERY STICKS, FINELY DICED

1 CARROT, PEELED AND FINELY DICED

2 GARLIC CLOVES, PEELED AND CHOPPED

1 CINNAMON STICK, BROKEN IN HALF

30 ML/2 TBSP GROUND ALMONDS

900 ML/1½ PINTS/3¾ CUPS HOT CHICKEN STOCK

SALT AND FRESHLY GROUND BLACK PEPPER

6 SLICES OF CIABATTA OR OTHER CRUSTY ITALIAN
 BREAD

SMALL PIECE OF PARMESAN OR PECORINO CHEESE,
 TO SERVE

Heat the olive oil in a large wide saucepan, add the onions, celery, carrot, garlic, cinnamon and almonds and cook on a low heat, partially covered with a lid, for 1 hour. Add the stock to the pan, stirring well, and heat through gently. Season to taste.

To serve, toast the slices of bread and place in 6 warmed soup bowls. Ladle the soup over and serve at once, with Parmesan or pecorino cheese to grate or shave on top.

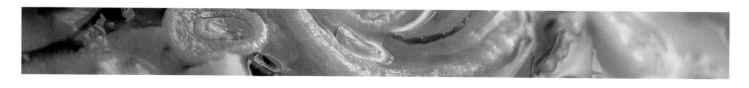

RIBOLLITA (TUSCAN BEAN SOUP)

Ribollita **is traditionally prepared in two stages, starting the day before it is to be eaten.**

Serves 6

THE BEANS

225 G/8 OZ/1¼ CUPS DRIED CANNELLINI BEANS
1 CELERY STICK, LEFT WHOLE
1 ONION, PEELED AND QUARTERED

2 GARLIC CLOVES, PEELED AND HALVED
SPRIG EACH OF FRESH SAGE AND ROSEMARY
SALT AND FRESHLY GROUND BLACK PEPPER

THE SOUP

60 ML/4 TBSP OLIVE OIL
1 LARGE ONION, PEELED AND CHOPPED
2.5 ML/½ TSP DRIED CHILLI FLAKES
3 RIPE TOMATOES, SKINNED, SEEDED AND CHOPPED
15 ML/1 TBSP TOMATO PURÉE
2 GARLIC CLOVES, PEELED AND CHOPPED
2 CARROTS, PEELED AND DICED

2 MEDIUM POTATOES, PEELED AND DICED
1 LEEK, CHOPPED
3 CELERY STICKS, FINELY CHOPPED
350 G/12 OZ SPRING GREENS OR OTHER GREEN
  CABBAGE, SHREDDED
LARGE SPRIG OF FRESH THYME

THE REHEATING

1 LARGE ONION, PEELED AND VERY THINLY SLICED
6 SLICES OF COUNTRY BREAD

2 GARLIC CLOVES, HALVED
45 ML/3 TBSP EXTRA VIRGIN OLIVE OIL

Soak the beans overnight in water to cover. Next day, drain them, rinse well and place in a saucepan with the celery, onion, garlic and herbs. Cover generously with cold water and bring to the boil. Cover the pan and leave to simmer for 1½ hours or until the beans are tender. Season with salt and pepper. Strain the beans, reserving the liquid, and discard the vegetables and herbs. Reserve a quarter of the beans. Purée the remaining beans using a food mill, blender or processor. Add water to the bean cooking liquid to make it up to 1.4 litres/2 ½ pints/6 cups.

To make the soup, heat the olive oil in a large ovenproof casserole dish, add the onion and chilli flakes and sauté for 5 minutes. Add the tomatoes, tomato purée and garlic and cook for 2–3 minutes, then stir in the puréed beans, all the vegetables and the thyme. Add the bean liquid, season and bring to the boil. Partially cover with a lid, lower the heat and cook very gently for 1½ hours, stirring occasionally. Turn off the heat and leave until the next day.

To reheat the soup, stir the reserved whole beans into it, then arrange the onion slices over the surface. Cook, uncovered, in an oven preheated to 180°C/350°F/Gas Mark 4 for about 1 hour, until it is hot and the onion is tender. Rub the bread slices with the garlic cloves and toast them under a hot grill (broiler) or on a ridged cast-iron grill pan until lightly browned. Put the bread slices in 6 soup bowls and ladle the hot soup over. Drizzle the extra virgin olive oil over each serving.

MUSSEL AND WHITE WINE SOUP

Perhaps not quite a soup, this is really a dish of mussels with a superb broth of white wine, fruity oil, garlic and tomato, served over slices of garlic toast made from good rustic bread. You could add some clams to it if they are available.

Serves 4

1.4 KG/3 LB MUSSELS

60 ML/4 TBSP OLIVE OIL

2 GARLIC CLOVES, PEELED AND CRUSHED

3 LARGE RIPE TOMATOES, SKINNED AND CHOPPED

300 ML/½ PINT/1¼ CUPS DRY WHITE WINE

45 ML/3 TBSP FINELY CHOPPED FRESH PARSLEY

SALT AND FRESHLY GROUND BLACK PEPPER

GARLIC TOAST

4 SLICES OF COUNTRY BREAD

2 GARLIC CLOVES, CUT IN HALF

45 ML/3 TBSP OLIVE OIL

COARSE SALT

Scrub the mussels and remove the beards, then rinse clean in plenty of fresh water. Discard any that do not close tightly when lightly tapped.

Put 1.25 cm/½ inch of water in a large saucepan and bring to the boil. Add the mussels, cover with a tight-fitting lid and cook over a high heat for 2–4 minutes until the shells have opened. Strain, reserving the cooking liquor. Discard any mussels that remain closed.

Heat the olive oil in a clean pan, add the garlic and cook for a few minutes until it begins to colour. Stir in the tomatoes and white wine, bring to the boil, then add the mussel liquor (poured in carefully to filter out any grit) and 15 ml/1 tbsp of the chopped parsley. Lower the heat and simmer gently for 15 minutes. Season to taste.

Just before serving, prepare the garlic toasts. Lightly toast the bread and rub the cut garlic cloves over one side of each slice. Brush with the olive oil and sprinkle with a little coarse salt. Return to the grill (broiler) for a few minutes until very hot.

To serve the soup, add the mussels to the broth and heat through. Place the garlic toast in 4 shallow soup bowls, ladle the mussel soup on top and serve at once, sprinkled with the remaining parsley.

WHITE BEAN 'CREMA' WITH OREGANO AND BAY

Tuscans are lucky enough to be able to obtain fresh cannellini beans in the summer months. So as not to mask their flavour, they might use them in a simple recipe such as this creamy soup. Fresh beans are unavailable here but you can still make a delicious version using dried ones. A thread of green virgin olive oil should be trickled over each serving.

Serves 4

350 G/12 OZ/2 CUPS DRIED CANNELLINI BEANS

1 BAY LEAF

1 ONION, PEELED AND HALVED

SPRIG OF FRESH OREGANO PLUS 15 ML/1 TBSP CHOPPED OREGANO

SALT AND FRESHLY GROUND BLACK PEPPER

60 ML/4 TBSP OLIVE OIL

2 GARLIC CLOVES, PEELED AND CHOPPED

EXTRA VIRGIN OLIVE OIL, TO SERVE

Soak the beans overnight in water to cover. The next day, drain and rinse the beans, then put them in a saucepan with the bay leaf, onion and oregano sprig. Cover with 1 litre/1¾ pints/4 cups of cold water and bring to the boil. Partially cover with a lid, lower the heat and simmer for 1–1½ hours, until the beans are tender. Pick out and discard the oregano sprig and the onion.

Using a slotted spoon, lift out about a quarter of the beans and set aside. Purée the rest of the soup by passing it through a food mill (this gets rid of the skins at the same time) or using a blender or food processor and then passing it through a sieve (not a fine one as this would be a great deal of trouble). Return the purée to the saucepan with the whole beans and season with lots of salt and pepper. Reheat gently.

Heat the olive oil in a separate pan and add the garlic, chopped oregano and a little seasoning. Fry gently until the garlic just begins to colour, then stir this mixture into the hot soup. Turn off the heat and leave to stand for a few minutes before serving trickled with a little extra virgin olive oil.

ANTIPASTI

CROSTINI WITH CHICKEN LIVERS AND CRISP FRIED SAGE

Appetizers like this are popular throughout Italy, served with a glass of chilled wine. The chicken liver topping is typically Tuscan.

Makes 12

225 G/8 OZ CHICKEN LIVERS, THAWED IF FROZEN

10 ML/2 TSP PLAIN WHITE FLOUR (ALL-PURPOSE FLOUR)

60 ML/4 TBSP OLIVE OIL

HANDFUL OF FRESH SAGE LEAVES

½ ONION, PEELED AND FINELY CHOPPED

2 GARLIC CLOVES, PEELED AND CRUSHED

45 ML/3 TBSP VIN SANTO OR MARSALA WINE

15 ML/1 TBSP BRANDY (OPTIONAL)

30 ML/2 TBSP CAPERS, DRAINED AND RINSED

4 PICKLED GHERKINS, FINELY CHOPPED

SALT AND FRESHLY GROUND BLACK PEPPER

12 THIN SLICES OF CIABATTA BREAD

Rinse the chicken livers and pat dry on kitchen paper. Dust lightly with the flour. Heat the olive oil in a deep frying pan (skillet). When very hot, add the sage leaves and let them frazzle for a few seconds only before transferring to a plate with a slotted spoon.

Add the onion and garlic to the pan, lower the heat and cook for about 5 minutes, until softened. Add the chicken livers and cook, stirring, for 2 minutes to seal. Pour in the wine and the brandy, if using, and cook for 3–4 minutes, until the chicken livers are tender; they should still be slightly pink on the outside. Add the capers and gherkins to the pan and remove from the heat.

Arrange the bread slices in a single layer on a baking sheet and toast in an oven preheated to 200°C/400°F/Gas Mark 6 for a few minutes, until golden. Meanwhile, transfer the chicken liver mixture to a food processor and blend to a coarse paste. Spread on to the hot crostini and serve at once, scattered with the fried sage leaves.

(Illustrated on pages 54-55)

MIXED SEAFOOD SALAD

Varying the fish from the ones suggested below would do no harm to this salad – look to the market and the fishmonger for inspiration and choose whatever is freshest. For me, the essentials are prawns and squid but the clams or mussels could be replaced with scallops, and some firm-textured fish could be included, too. Serve with other antipasti or as a light, summery main course.

Serves 4	450 G/1 LB CLAMS OR MUSSELS IN THEIR SHELLS	1 GARLIC CLOVE, PEELED AND CRUSHED
as a main	450 G/1 LB SQUID	5 ML/1 TSP FINELY GRATED LEMON ZEST
course	350 G/12 OZ LARGE PRAWNS (SHRIMP), PREFERABLY	JUICE OF 1 LEMON
Serves 8	RAW	HANDFUL OF FRESH PARSLEY, CHOPPED
as a starter	90 ML/6 TBSP OLIVE OIL	SALT AND FRESHLY GROUND BLACK PEPPER

Scrub the clams or mussels, removing the beards from mussels, then rinse clean in plenty of fresh water. Discard any that do not close tightly when lightly tapped. Put 1.25 cm/½ inch of water in a large saucepan and bring to the boil. Add the clams or mussels, cover with a tight-fitting lid and cook over a high heat for 2–4 minutes until the shells have opened. Strain, reserving the cooking liquor. Discard any clams or mussels that remain closed. Leave to cool.

Clean the squid and slice the body parts into rings. Leave small tentacles whole but cut them up if they are large. Peel and de-vein the prawns (shrimp). Place both the squid and prawns (shrimp) in a bowl with 30 ml/2 tbsp of the olive oil and the garlic. Mix well.

Preheat a dry cast-iron grill pan over a high heat for 5 minutes. Pick out the squid from the bowl and place on the grill. Allow to sizzle undisturbed for 1 minute, then turn and cook for another minute or until tender. (You may have to cook them in batches.) Transfer to a bowl. Cook the prawns for 1 minute per side in the same way and add to the cooked squid.

Remove the shells from most of the clams or mussels for ease of eating. Add all the clams or mussels to the other seafood, together with the lemon zest and juice, the parsley and the remaining olive oil. Season with salt and pepper and mix well. Leave to stand for at least 30 minutes before serving.

ASPARAGUS, BROAD BEAN (FAVA BEAN) AND PARMESAN FRITTATA

Serves 2–4

225 G/8 OZ ASPARAGUS, TRIMMED
1 LARGE POTATO, PEELED
225 G/8 OZ/1⅓ CUPS FRESH OR THAWED FROZEN
   BROAD BEANS (FAVA BEANS)
6 EGGS

SALT AND FRESHLY GROUND BLACK PEPPER
50 G/2 OZ/⅔ CUP PARMESAN CHEESE, FRESHLY
   GRATED
45 ML/3 TBSP CHOPPED FRESH MIXED HERBS
40 G/1½ OZ/3 TBSP BUTTER

Steam the asparagus for 12 minutes or until tender, then plunge it into cold water to set the colour. Leave to cool completely, then cut it into short lengths. Cook the potato in boiling salted water for 15-20 minutes or until tender. Cool and then dice. If using fresh broad beans (fava beans), blanch for 1 minute, then drain. Slip the broad beans (fava beans) out of their skins.

Beat the eggs together with a good pinch of salt, a lot of pepper and half the Parmesan cheese. Stir in the asparagus, beans and herbs. Melt the butter in a 22.5-cm/10-inch heavy non-stick frying pan (skillet). When foaming, pour in the egg mixture, turn down the heat as low as possible and cook for about 15 minutes, until the omelette is set underneath but still a little runny on top. Scatter over the cooked diced potato and sprinkle with the remaining Parmesan cheese. Place under a hot grill (broiler) until the top is just set and the cheese is lightly browned. It should not brown too much or it will dry out. Slide on to a warm plate and cut into wedges to serve.

OVERLEAF: (FRONT) CROSTINI WITH CHICKEN LIVERS AND CRISP-FRIED SAGE (P.49)
(BACK) BRUSCHETTA AL POMODORO

ARTICHOKE FRITTATA WITH PORCINI OR TRUFFLES

Flat omelettes like this one are popular in Tuscany and indeed all over Italy. Similar to a Spanish omelette, they are fairly substantial and contain plenty of vegetables and other ingredients as well as eggs. This recipe uses dried porcini mushrooms but if you are lucky enough to get hold of fresh black truffles this would be a good dish in which to use them. In this event, omit the porcini.

Serves 4–6

15 G/½ OZ/½ CUP DRIED PORCINI MUSHROOMS

3 SMALL-TO-MEDIUM ARTICHOKES

LEMON JUICE

ABOUT 10 ML/2 TSP PLAIN WHITE FLOUR (ALL-PURPOSE FLOUR)

60 ML/4 TBSP OLIVE OIL

40 G/1½ OZ/3 TBSP BUTTER

6 EGGS, BEATEN

SALT AND FRESHLY GROUND BLACK PEPPER

Place the porcini in a small bowl, cover with boiling water and leave to soak while you prepare the artichokes.

Trim off all the hard outer leaves from the artichokes and slice off about two-thirds of the tops. Scoop out the chokes, using a teaspoon, and then thinly slice the bases, rubbing them with lemon juice to prevent discoloration. Coat them in the flour. Heat the oil in a large deep frying pan (skillet), add the artichoke slices and sauté for a few minutes, until tender.

Meanwhile remove the porcini from their liquid and chop them finely. Add to the pan and continue cooking for a minute or two. Add the butter to the pan and heat until sizzling. Pour in the beaten eggs and add some seasoning. Tilt the pan so the mixture covers the base and cook gently, pushing the set egg mixture at the edge of the pan into the centre and tilting the pan as you go. When the frittata is almost set, after about 5 minutes, continue cooking until the base is lightly browned, then finish off the top with a few seconds under a hot grill (broiler). Serve hot, warm or at room temperature.

BRUSCHETTA AL POMODORO

Make this with lovely ripe fresh tomatoes and some good bread. As well as antipasti, bruschetta also makes an unbeatable lunch with some prosciutto, a few olives and a glass of Chianti.

Serves 8

8 SLICES OF CRUSTY BREAD (CIABATTA WILL DO BUT SOMETHING A LITTLE MORE RUSTIC IS PREFERABLE)

2 GARLIC CLOVES, CUT IN HALF

150 ML/¼ PINT/⅔ CUP OLIVE OIL

3 LARGE RIPE TOMATOES, SLICED

15 ML/1 TBSP FRESH BASIL LEAVES

SALT AND FRESHLY GROUND BLACK PEPPER

Toast the bread on both sides under a hot grill (broiler). Rub the cut garlic cloves over the hot toast and drizzle about half the oil over it. Top the toast with the tomato slices and sprinkle with the basil and plenty of salt and pepper. Drizzle the remaining olive oil over the tomatoes and return to the grill (broiler) to heat through before serving.

SPRING VEGETABLE CRUDITÉS WITH EXTRA VIRGIN OLIVE OIL

Extra virgin olive oil is by far the favourite sauce of Tuscany, whether it is the delicate golden oil of Lucca that many claim is superior or a bolder, greener version from the Chianti hills. Here it is served as a dip for an assortment of raw and lightly cooked spring vegetables.

Serves 4

1 BUNCH OF BABY FENNEL, LEFT WHOLE, OR 2 FENNEL BULBS, HALVED LENGTHWISE

1 BUNCH OF BABY CARROTS, LEFT WHOLE, OR 4 LARGE CARROTS, HALVED LENGTHWISE

4 CELERY STICKS, CUT INTO LONG THIN STRIPS

1 BUNCH OF ASPARAGUS, TRIMMED

8 SPRING ONIONS (SCALLIONS), TRIMMED

4 BABY CUCUMBERS OR 1 LARGE CUCUMBER, CUT INTO LONG THIN STRIPS

150 ML/¼ PINT /⅔ CUP EXTRA VIRGIN OLIVE OIL

FINE SEA SALT AND FRESHLY GROUND BLACK PEPPER

Bring a large pan of salted water to the boil and add the fennel, carrots, celery and asparagus. Bring back to the boil and cook for 2–3 minutes, then drain and refresh under cold running water. Drain again thoroughly.

Arrange all the vegetables on a platter or stand them up in a deep serving dish. Beat the olive oil with salt and pepper and serve in individual shallow bowls for dipping.

CROSTINI WITH PORK AND FRIED QUAIL'S EGGS

Use a small, thin loaf such as a baguette to make the crostini, or cut larger slices into small squares.

Serves 4–6

175 G/6 OZ PORK TENDERLOIN

COARSE SEA SALT AND FRESHLY GROUND BLACK PEPPER

12 SMALL SLICES CRUSTY BREAD, 1 CM/⅓ INCH THICK

75 ML/5 TBSP EXTRA VIRGIN OLIVE OIL

12 QUAIL'S EGGS

½ LEMON

Cut the pork into 12 thin slices and flatten each slightly with a rolling pin or meat mallet. Season the pork slices lightly with pepper.

Arrange the bread on a baking sheet and drizzle over 30 ml/2 tbsp of the olive oil. Grill (broil) on both sides until lightly golden. Keep warm. Heat 15 ml/1 tbsp of the remaining oil in a large frying pan (skillet) until very hot. Add the pork slices and cook for a few seconds only on each side, then transfer them to a warm plate and lower the heat a little.

Add the remaining oil to the pan and crack in the quail's eggs – you may find it easier to cook them in 3 batches. While they are frying, place one slice of cooked pork on each slice of bread and squeeze a drop or two of lemon juice over it.

Top the crostini with the fried eggs and serve at once, sprinkled with a little coarse salt.

PASTA, RICE AND GRAINS
PAPPARDELLE WITH RABBIT AND WILD MUSHROOMS

Based on the classic Tuscan dish, pappardelle with hare, this could also be made with chicken thigh meat, if you prefer. Rigatoni or penne can be substituted for the pappardelle.

Serves 4

15 G/½ OZ/1 TBSP BUTTER

75 ML/5 TBSP OLIVE OIL

1 SMALL ONION, PEELED AND FINELY CHOPPED

1 LARGE CARROT, PEELED AND FINELY DICED

1 CELERY STICK, FINELY DICED

350 G/12 OZ BONELESS RABBIT, CUT INTO SMALL DICE

10 ML/2 TSP CHOPPED FRESH ROSEMARY

15 ML/1 TBSP JUNIPER BERRIES, LIGHTLY CRUSHED

1 GLASS OF RED WINE

400 G/14 OZ CAN OF PLUM TOMATOES IN JUICE, CHOPPED

1 GARLIC CLOVE, PEELED AND CRUSHED

ABOUT 225 G/8 OZ FLAT FIELD MUSHROOMS OR OTHER WILD MUSHROOMS, ROUGHLY CHOPPED

SALT AND FRESHLY GROUND BLACK PEPPER

350 G/12 OZ PAPPARDELLE

FRESHLY GRATED PARMESAN CHEESE, TO SERVE

Heat the butter and 30 ml/2 tbsp of the olive oil in a large saucepan, add the onion and sauté over a medium heat for about 5 minutes, until softened. Stir in the carrot and celery and cook for a further 7–8 minutes, until the vegetables have softened and are beginning to colour. Add the rabbit, rosemary and juniper berries to the pan and turn up the heat to brown the meat. Pour in the wine and let it bubble until most of it has evaporated. Add the tomatoes and their juice to the pan with a little seasoning. Bring to the boil, then lower the heat so the sauce is barely simmering. Cover and cook for 45 minutes or until the rabbit is tender.

Heat the remaining olive oil in a frying pan (skillet), add the garlic and sauté for 1 minute. Add the mushrooms and cook, stirring, for a few minutes until the mushrooms are tender. Season with salt and pepper. Add this mixture to the pan of rabbit sauce but do not stir it in.

Cook the pasta in a large pan of boiling salted water until *al dente* and then drain thoroughly. Toss with the rabbit sauce in a heated serving bowl and serve sprinkled with freshly grated Parmesan cheese.

SPAGHETTI AND FRESH TOMATO SAUCE

The heat from the pasta releases the delicious flavours of this sauce. Only use really ripe tomatoes.

Serves 4

4 LARGE, RIPE TOMATOES, ABOUT 700 G/1½ LB

2 GARLIC CLOVES, PEELED AND FINELY CHOPPED

60 ML/4 TBSP CHOPPED FRESH BASIL

150 ML/¼ PINT/⅔ CUP EXTRA VIRGIN OLIVE OIL

SALT AND FRESHLY GROUND BLACK PEPPER

450 G/1 LB SPAGHETTI

CHOPPED FRESH HERBS, TO SERVE

To skin the tomatoes place them in boiling water for 1 minute, then lift out with a slotted spoon and plunge into cold water. Peel and halve the tomatoes and squeeze out the seeds. Dice into 5 mm/¼ inch cubes and mix with the garlic, basil, oil and seasoning in a non-metallic bowl. Cover and leave for at least half an hour for the flavours to mellow. Cook the pasta in plenty of boiling salted water until *al dente*, then drain leaving a tablespoon of the cooking water in the pan with the pasta. Mix in the sauce, cover with a lid and leave for 2–3 minutes. Toss again and serve immediately, garnished with fresh herbs.

HERB RISOTTO

A simple risotto, without pretension but full of character and flavour.

**Serves 4
as a starter**

750 ML/1¼ PINTS/3 CUPS WELL-FLAVOURED CHICKEN
   OR VEGETABLE STOCK

50 G/2 OZ/¼ CUP BUTTER

2 SHALLOTS, PEELED AND FINELY CHOPPED

225 G/8 OZ/1⅛ CUPS ITALIAN RISOTTO RICE

30 ML/2 TBSP CHOPPED FRESH THYME

30 ML/2 TBSP CHOPPED FRESH SAGE

30 ML/2 TBSP CHOPPED FRESH OREGANO

60 ML/4 TBSP FINELY GRATED PECORINO CHEESE

HANDFUL OF FRESH BASIL LEAVES, ROUGHLY TORN

SALT AND FRESHLY GROUND BLACK PEPPER

PECORINO OR PARMESAN CHEESE, TO SERVE

Heat the stock to simmering point; keep it simmering gently while you make the risotto. Melt about half the butter in a medium saucepan. Add the shallots and cook, stirring, for a few minutes until softened. Add the rice and stir for a few minutes until translucent. Pour about half the hot stock into the pan and stir for 8–10 minutes until it is almost completely absorbed. Add about half the remaining stock and stir again until absorbed. Add the thyme, sage and oregano to the pan with the last of the stock. Cook, stirring gently, until the risotto is creamy and the grains of rice are tender, then add the remaining butter, grated pecorino and basil to the pan and season. Serve immediately, with extra pecorino or parmesan cheese shaved over.

SPAGHETTI WITH PRAWNS AND CHILLI

Serves 4–6

1 KG/2¼ LB COOKED LARGE PRAWNS (SHRIMP) IN
    THEIR SHELLS
A FEW PARSLEY STALKS
1 CARROT, PEELED AND CHOPPED
1 CELERY STICK, CHOPPED
1 SMALL ONION, PEELED AND QUARTERED
SALT AND FRESHLY GROUND BLACK PEPPER

60 ML/4 TBSP OLIVE OIL
2 GARLIC CLOVES, PEELED AND CRUSHED
2.5 ML/½ TSP DRIED CHILLI FLAKES
4 TOMATOES, SKINNED, SEEDED AND CHOPPED
1 GLASS OF DRY WHITE WINE
30 ML/2 TBSP CHOPPED FRESH PARSLEY
400 G/14 OZ SPAGHETTI

First, make a fish stock: peel the prawns (shrimp), keeping the shells and heads. Set the tails aside. Place the shells and heads in a saucepan with the parsley stalks, carrot, celery and onion. Add about 1 litre/1¾ pints/4 cups of water, season and bring to the boil. Lower the heat, cover and simmer for 30 minutes, then strain.

To prepare the sauce, chop the prawn (shrimp) tails. Heat the olive oil in a large sauté pan, add the garlic and chilli flakes and cook until the garlic begins to colour. Stir in the tomatoes and cook for 1 minute, then add the white wine and bring to the boil. Leave to bubble gently, uncovered, for 3–4 minutes, then add the chopped parsley and a ladleful of the fish stock to the pan. Return to the boil, then stir in the prawns (shrimp) and remove from the heat. Adjust the seasoning to taste.

Cook the spaghetti in the remaining fish stock, topped up with water if necessary, until *al dente*. Drain thoroughly. Serve the spaghetti in warmed bowls with the hot sauce spooned over.

POLENTA WITH MASCARPONE AND MUSHROOMS

A 'loose' polenta dish flavoured with pecorino cheese and served with a dollop of cool mascarpone and cooked mushrooms.

15 G/½ OZ/½ CUP DRIED PORCINI MUSHROOMS

40 G/1½ OZ/3 TBSP BUTTER

30 ML/2 TBSP OLIVE OIL

1 GARLIC CLOVE, PEELED AND CRUSHED

15 ML/1 TBSP CHOPPED FRESH THYME

2 LARGE RIPE TOMATOES, SKINNED AND CHOPPED

600 G/1¼ LB MIXED FRESH MUSHROOMS, SLICED IF LARGE

COARSE SEA SALT AND FRESHLY GROUND BLACK PEPPER

8 HEAPED TBSP MASCARPONE

POLENTA 2.5 ML/½ TSP SALT

225 G/8 OZ/2 CUPS POLENTA (CORNMEAL)

25 G/1 OZ/2 TBSP BUTTER

60 ML/4 TBSP FINELY GRATED PECORINO CHEESE

Place the porcini in a small bowl, cover with boiling water and leave to soak while you prepare the polenta.

Bring 1.4 litres/2½ pints/6 cups water to a rolling boil in a large pot. Add the salt and then sprinkle the polenta gradually into the pan, stirring constantly with a wooden spoon. Lower the heat and cook, stirring constantly, for about 20 minutes or according to the instructions on the packet, until the polenta is thick and smooth. Remove from the heat and stir in the butter and pecorino cheese. Adjust the seasoning and keep hot.

Drain and finely chop the porcini. Heat the butter and oil in a large frying pan (skillet), add the garlic and thyme and cook gently for 2–3 minutes. Add the tomatoes, fresh mushrooms and porcini and cook, stirring, over a medium heat for 8–10 minutes, until tender. Season with coarse salt and freshly ground black pepper.

To serve, pile the polenta on to 4 warmed serving plates and dollop the mascarpone on top. Spoon the mushroom mixture on top of that and serve at once.

HAND-MADE TAGLIARINI WITH OLIVE OIL AND GARLIC

Quality and simplicity are paramount in this dish, designed to test the new season's olive oil. You'll need a pasta machine to roll and cut the pasta.

Serves 4

2 GARLIC CLOVES, HALVED

ABOUT 100 ML/4 FL OZ EXTRA VIRGIN OLIVE OIL

45 ML/3 TBSP FINELY GRATED PECORINO CHEESE

FRESHLY GROUND BLACK PEPPER

10 ML/2 TSP FINELY CHOPPED FRESH PARSLEY, TO GARNISH

PASTA

300 G/10 OZ/2½ CUPS '00' PASTA FLOUR (OR ALL-PURPOSE FLOUR)

PINCH OF SALT

3 SIZE-3 (MEDIUM) EGGS

To make the pasta, sift the flour and salt on to a clean work surface or board, make a large well in the centre and break the eggs into the well. Use a fork to beat the eggs together, gradually drawing in the flour and taking care not to let the egg escape from the flour well. When the mixture begins to thicken to a soft paste, use your hands to mix to a firm dough. Knead on a clean surface for 5 minutes, until smooth and velvety. Wrap in cling film (plastic wrap) to prevent drying out and leave to rest for 10–15 minutes.

Using a pasta machine, roll out the dough in batches until you reach the penultimate setting on the machine. Cut into ribbons according to the manufacturer's instructions. Lay the pasta loosely on a clean towel until ready to cook.

To cook the pasta, bring a large pan of salted water to the boil, add the pasta and return to the boil. Cook until *al dente* – this can take anything from 30 seconds to 2 minutes, depending on the thickness of the pasta and how much it has dried, so keep testing it. Drain thoroughly.

Rub the cut surface of the garlic cloves all around the inside of a serving bowl. Add the pasta to the bowl and cover with the olive oil and grated pecorino cheese. Season with black pepper and toss lightly. Serve at once, sprinkled with the chopped parsley.

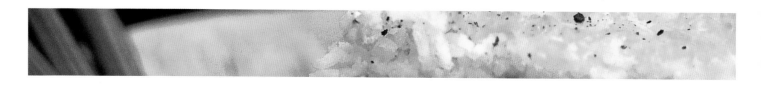

RICE AND CHEESE CAKE WITH TOMATO AND VEGETABLE SAUCE

Serves 6

RICE CAKE

450 G/1 LB/2¼ CUPS LONG GRAIN RICE	350 G/12 OZ TALEGGIO CHEESE, SLICED
125 G/4 OZ/½ CUP BUTTER	SALT AND FRESHLY GROUND BLACK PEPPER
75 G/3 OZ/¾ CUP PECORINO CHEESE, FINELY GRATED	FRESHLY GRATED NUTMEG

SAUCE

1 KG/2¼ LB RIPE TOMATOES	15 ML/1 TBSP CHOPPED FRESH BASIL
1 ONION, PEELED AND FINELY CHOPPED	45 ML/3 TBSP OLIVE OIL
1 CARROT, PEELED AND FINELY CHOPPED	SALT AND FRESHLY GROUND BLACK PEPPER
1 CELERY STICK, FINELY CHOPPED	

First make the sauce. Peel the tomatoes by plunging them into boiling water for 20 seconds, then transferring to a bowl of cold water with a slotted spoon. Slip off the skins and quarter the tomatoes, removing the hard cores. Put all the sauce ingredients in a saucepan and bring to the boil, then cover and simmer for 30 minutes. Remove the lid and simmer for about 20 minutes, until reduced and thick. Purée in a blender or food processor or press through a sieve, then season to taste. Reheat before serving.

Generously butter a deep 20-cm/8-inch spring-form cake tin (cake pan). Cook the rice in boiling salted water for about 10 minutes, until just tender, then drain thoroughly in a colander. Place in a bowl with the butter, cut into small pieces, and the grated pecorino. Toss lightly to mix.

Spread about a quarter of the rice over the base of the prepared tin (pan) and cover with about a third of the Taleggio cheese. Season with a little salt, pepper and nutmeg. Cover the cheese with another layer of rice and continue these layers to use up all the cheese and rice, finishing with a layer of rice. Bake for about 25 minutes in an oven preheated to 180°C/350°F/Gas Mark 4, until the rice is tender and the cake is a golden colour. Cool slightly before turning out and serving with the sauce.

FISH

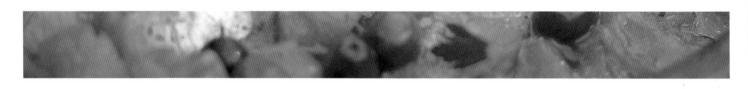

BRAISED RED MULLET

Serves 4

FOUR 225 G/8 OZ RED MULLET, CLEANED AND
SCALED
450G/1LB RIPE TOMATOES, SKINNED, SEEDED AND
CHOPPED
90 ML/6 TBSP EXTRA VIRGIN OLIVE OIL

1 SMALL GLASS OF DRY WHITE WINE
3 GARLIC CLOVES, PEELED AND FINELY CHOPPED
50 G/2 OZ/⅓ CUP SMALL BLACK OLIVES
SALT AND FRESHLY GROUND BLACK PEPPER
CHOPPED FRESH PARSLEY, TO SERVE

Arrange the fish in a single layer in a large baking dish. Add the tomatoes and pour over the oil and wine. Scatter the garlic and olives over the top, then cover the dish with aluminium foil and bake in an oven preheated to 180°C/350°F/Gas Mark 4 for about 20-25 minutes or until the fish is firm and flakes easily. Serve straight from the dish, sprinkled with chopped parsley.

BAKED SEA BASS WITH BASIL AND CAPERS

Serves 4

LARGE BUNCH OF FRESH BASIL (ABOUT 75 G/3 OZ)
2 GARLIC CLOVES, PEELED AND CHOPPED
45 ML/3 TBSP CAPERS IN VINEGAR, RINSED AND
  DRAINED
SALT AND FRESHLY GROUND BLACK PEPPER

I SEA BASS, ABOUT 1.2 KG/2½ LB, SCALED AND
  CLEANED
ABOUT 60 ML/4 TBSP EXTRA VIRGIN OLIVE OIL
LEMON WEDGES, TO SERVE

Set aside a couple of basil sprigs to stuff the fish. Chop the rest together with the garlic, capers and a little seasoning to give a coarse paste. Make a long, deep cut in the flesh of each side of the sea bass from the head to the tail. Use half the basil, garlic and caper mixture to stuff one cut side and then lay the fish stuffed-side down in an oiled baking dish. Fill the other cut with the remaining stuffing, piling any excess down the top of the fish. Stuff the stomach cavity of the fish with the reserved basil sprigs and season the fish with salt and pepper. Drizzle the olive oil over and around the fish and cover lightly with foil. Bake for about 40 minutes in an oven preheated to 180°C/350°F/Gas Mark 4, removing the foil halfway through cooking. The flesh of the fish should flake easily when done. Serve at once, with lemon wedges.

SKEWERED AND GRILLED TUNA, PEPPERS AND ONIONS

Here the tuna is sliced wafer thin and marinated before rolling up and securing on skewers with vegetables for grilling.

Serves 4

450 G/1 LB FRESH TUNA STEAK

JUICE OF 1 LEMON

ABOUT 90 ML/6 TBSP EXTRA VIRGIN OLIVE OIL, PLUS
    EXTRA FOR BRUSHING

15 ML/1 TBSP CHOPPED FRESH THYME

15 ML/1 TBSP CHOPPED FRESH PARSLEY

SALT AND FRESHLY GROUND BLACK PEPPER

3 SMALL ONIONS, PEELED AND QUARTERED, LEAVING
    THE ROOT END INTACT

2 SWEET RED PEPPERS, HALVED AND SEEDED

16 BAY LEAVES

Slice the tuna as thinly as possible with a very sharp knife and cut into strips about 5 cm/2 inches wide. Place in a shallow dish with the lemon juice, 60 ml/4 tbsp of the olive oil, herbs and seasoning. Turn the pieces to coat, then cover and leave to marinate for about 30 minutes.

Meanwhile, arrange the onions on the grill pan (broiler pan) with the sweet red peppers, skin side up. Brush with a little oil and grill (broil) for about 5 minutes, until the skin of the peppers is blistered and blackened. Turn the onions as necessary to prevent them from burning. At this stage the onions should be only partly cooked. Leave the vegetables to cool slightly.

When the peppers are cool enough to handle, peel them and cut each piece lengthwise into 3, giving wide strips.

To assemble the skewers, remove the tuna from the marinade, roll up each piece and thread on to skewers, alternating with the onion, peppers and bay leaves. Cook under a hot grill (broiler) for about 6 minutes, turning occasionally and basting with any remaining marinade, until the fish is just cooked through. Take care not to overcook – the tuna should be moist and succulent. Serve hot, with a salad or vegetables.

RED AND YELLOW PEPPERS STUFFED WITH MONKFISH

Serves 4

2 SWEET RED PEPPERS
2 SWEET YELLOW PEPPERS
600 G/1¼ LB MONKFISH (ANGLER FISH) FILLET
60 ML/4 TBSP EXTRA VIRGIN OLIVE OIL
2 GARLIC CLOVES, PEELED AND CHOPPED

1 ONION, PEELED AND FINELY SLICED
½ GLASS OF DRY WHITE WINE
LARGE BUNCH OF FRESH BASIL, STALKS REMOVED
SALT AND FRESHLY GROUND BLACK PEPPER

Cut the peppers in half lengthwise and remove the seeds, leaving the stalks intact. Arrange skin-side down in a large baking dish and bake in an oven preheated to 180°C/350°F/Gas Mark 4 for about 20 minutes, until just tender.

Meanwhile, cut the monkfish into good bite-sized chunks. Heat the olive oil in a large shallow pan and cook the garlic and onion over a medium-high heat until softened and beginning to colour. Stir in the monkfish and cook until sealed on all sides. Pour in the wine and let it bubble for 1 minute, then add the basil leaves and stir until wilted. Remove the pan from the heat.

Divide the fish mixture between the roasted peppers. Season each with a little salt and pepper, then cover with aluminium foil and return to the oven for 15 minutes or until the monkfish is cooked through. Serve hot.

MEAT AND POULTRY

BEEF STEWED IN CHIANTI WITH SHALLOTS, ROSEMARY AND SPICES

Serves 4

60 ML/4 TBSP OLIVE OIL

12 SHALLOTS, PEELED

3 GARLIC CLOVES, PEELED AND CHOPPED

3 SPRIGS OF FRESH ROSEMARY

1 KG/2¼ LB BRAISING BEEF, CUT INTO CUBES

22.5 ML/1½ TBSP PLAIN WHITE FLOUR (ALL-PURPOSE FLOUR)

200 ML/7 FL OZ/⅞ CUP CHIANTI

400 G/14 OZ CAN OF PLUM TOMATOES, SEEDED AND CHOPPED

4 CLOVES

1 CINNAMON STICK, HALVED

SALT AND FRESHLY GROUND BLACK PEPPER

ABOUT 150 ML/¼ PINT/⅔ CUP BEEF STOCK, IF NECESSARY

Heat the oil in a large saucepan, add the shallots and brown them over a high heat for a few minutes. Remove with a slotted spoon and set aside. Add the garlic and rosemary to the pan and cook over a medium heat for 5 minutes. Dust the beef with the flour, add to the pan and cooking for 2–3 minutes, until browned.

Add the Chianti to the pan and stir well with a wooden spoon to scrape up all the sediment from the base of the pan. Bring to the boil and leave to bubble for a minute to boil off the alcohol. Stir in the tomatoes and their juice, plus the cloves, cinnamon and a little seasoning. Cover the pan with a tight-fitting lid and cook gently for 1¼ hours, stirring occasionally.

Check the level of liquid in the pan; if the beef looks in danger of drying out, add a little beef stock. Add the shallots to the pan, cover and continue cooking for 1 hour or until the meat is very tender. Adjust the seasoning and serve hot with potatoes and another vegetable.

CHAR-GRILLED STEAK WITH VEGETABLES

The Tuscans have a reputation as producers of fine beef and a tendency to prepare it almost puritanically, with very little in the way of sauces and flavourings that might disguise its quality. Here, a simply grilled fillet steak is serve on a bed of finely chopped vegetables that have been cooked in olive oil with garlic until meltingly tender.

Serves 4

FOUR 175 G/6 OZ FILLET STEAKS, ABOUT 4 CM/1½
    INCHES THICK
45 ML/3 TBSP OLIVE OIL, PLUS EXTRA FOR BRUSHING
SALT AND FRESHLY GROUND BLACK PEPPER
1 ONION, PEELED AND CHOPPED
2 GARLIC CLOVES, PEELED AND CHOPPED

2 CARROTS, PEELED AND DICED
2 CELERY STICKS OR 1 SMALL FENNEL BULB, DICED
3 LARGE RIPE TOMATOES, SKINNED, SEEDED AND
    CHOPPED
TORN FLAT-LEAF PARSLEY, TO GARNISH

Brush the steaks with olive oil and season with coarsely ground black pepper. To prepare the vegetables, heat the olive oil in a large saucepan, add the onion and garlic and cook for a few minutes, until softened but not browned. Stir in the carrots and celery or fennel, then cover and cook for 10 minutes over a medium-high heat. Add the tomatoes and seasoning, cover and continue cooking for 5 minutes.

Cook the steaks over charcoal (or under a preheated grill) for about 6 minutes, turning once. This will give medium rare meat – you can alter the cooking time according to preference.

Serve the steaks at once on a bed of the vegetables, scattered with a little torn parsley to garnish.

PORK AND FENNEL SAUSAGES SKEWERED WITH BREAD AND VEGETABLES

Pork and fennel sausages are available from Italian delicatessens but you can use any well-flavoured sausage for these kebabs, dividing them into small links to fit on the skewers. Serve with a salad or with a Tuscan dish of white beans (see page 87).

Serves 4

450 G/1 LB PORK AND FENNEL SAUSAGES

1 BAGUETTE, CUT INTO SLICES 1 CM/⅓ INCH THICK

2 GARLIC CLOVES, PEELED AND CRUSHED

75 ML/5 TBSP OLIVE OIL

5 ML/1 TSP FENNEL SEEDS, CRUSHED

COARSE SALT AND FRESHLY GROUND BLACK PEPPER

6 SHALLOTS, PEELED AND HALVED

6 BABY FENNEL BULBS, HALVED

1 YELLOW PEPPER, CUT INTO LARGE DICE

ABOUT 8 BAY LEAVES

Divide the sausages into smaller ones about 5 cm/2 inches long. Arrange the slices of bread in a single layer on a board or baking sheet. Put the garlic, olive oil and fennel seeds in a small saucepan and heat gently for a few minutes but do not allow the garlic to brown. Drizzle this mixture over the bread, then season with salt and pepper. Blanch the shallots, fennel and yellow pepper in a pan of boiling water for 1 minute, then drain thoroughly. Thread the sausages, bread, vegetables and bay leaves on to 4 long skewers. Arrange on a baking sheet or in an ovenproof shallow dish and bake for about 15 minutes in an oven preheated to 200°C/400°F/Gas Mark 6, turning once, until the sausages are cooked through and the vegetables are tender. The bread should be crisp and browned. Serve hot.

ROAST LEG OF LAMB WITH GARLIC, ROSEMARY, WINE AND BAY

Ask your butcher partially to bone the leg of lamb leaving only the end piece of bone, which is useful to hold on to while carving.

Serves 6

LEG OF LAMB, PARTIALLY BONED (ABOUT 1.4 KG/ 3 LB WEIGHT AFTER BONING)

2 GARLIC CLOVES, PEELED AND CHOPPED

15 ML/1 TBSP CHOPPED FRESH ROSEMARY

60 ML/4 TBSP OLIVE OIL

SALT AND FRESHLY GROUND BLACK PEPPER

2 LARGE SPRIGS OF FRESH BAY LEAVES

1 GLASS OF WHITE WINE

Lay the leg of lamb out flat and sprinkle the inside with the chopped garlic and rosemary and half the oil. Season generously with salt and pepper and roll up neatly to enclose the seasonings. Tie with string to secure.

Put the lamb in a roasting tin (roasting pan) and tuck the bay sprigs underneath. Rub the remaining oil over the lamb and pour in the wine. Roast for 15 minutes in an oven preheated to 230°C/450°F/Gas Mark 8, then reduce the temperature to 200°C/400°F/Gas Mark 6 and continue roasting for 1 hour, basting occasionally. The lamb should be slightly pink at this stage; if you prefer it well done, cook for another 15 minutes. Leave the lamb to rest for 15 minutes before carving. Serve thickly sliced with the pan juices, skimmed of fat, spooned over.

ROAST LOIN OF PORK WITH BEANS

This dish relies heavily on the strong flavours of garlic, rosemary, salt and pepper. To achieve a true Tuscan flavour, do not stint on the salt and pepper!

Serves 6

5 GARLIC CLOVES, PEELED

30 ML/2 TBSP CHOPPED FRESH ROSEMARY

SALT AND FRESHLY GROUND BLACK PEPPER

1.4 KG/3 LB BONED PORK LOIN (NO RIND)

90 ML/6 TBSP OLIVE OIL

150 ML/¼ PINT/⅔ CUP WHITE WINE

3-4 FRESH SAGE LEAVES

1 KG/2¼ LB FRESH HARICOT BEANS (NAVY BEANS), SHELLED, OR TWO 400 G/14 OZ CANS HARICOT BEANS (NAVY BEANS), DRAINED

400 G/14 OZ CAN CHOPPED TOMATOES

Chop 2 of the garlic cloves and mix with the rosemary and 5 ml/1 tsp each of salt and pepper. Pierce the meat deeply all over with a thin, sharp knife and push the rosemary mixture into the slits. Roll up the meat and tie at regular intervals. Rub all over with 45 ml/3 tbsp of the olive oil and season well. Place in a roasting tin (roasting pan), pour in the wine and bake in an oven preheated to 160°C/325°F/Gas Mark 3 for about 1½ hours, basting frequently.

Slice the remaining garlic cloves. Heat the remaining oil and add the sliced garlic and the sage. Fry gently until golden, then add the beans. Stir, then add the tomatoes. Season well with black pepper and bring to the boil. Pour around the meat and bake for a further 30–45 minutes, until the meat is tender and the beans cooked.

DUCKLING WITH PINE NUTS, RAISINS AND ORANGE

You might find it easier to buy duckling pieces for this dish – legs or breasts as you prefer – although it will certainly be cheaper to use a whole bird.

Serves 4

1 OVEN-READY DUCKLING, JOINTED	2 WHOLE CLOVES
30 ML/2 TBSP OLIVE OIL	300 ML/½ PINT/1¼ CUPS RED WINE
1 ONION, PEELED AND CHOPPED	1 LARGE ORANGE
1 GARLIC CLOVE, PEELED AND CHOPPED	SALT AND FRESHLY GROUND BLACK PEPPER
1 CARROT, PEELED AND FINELY DICED	25 G/1 OZ/¼ CUP PINE NUTS, TOASTED
1 CELERY STICK, FINELY DICED	60 ML/4 TBSP BRANDY
50 G/2 OZ/⅓ CUP RAISINS	

Remove all the skin from the duck pieces (this will take with it all the fat). Heat the olive oil in a large sauté pan, add the onion and garlic and cook over a medium heat for 5 minutes, until softened. Stir in the carrot and celery and continue cooking for 5 minutes.

Add the duck pieces, raisins, cloves and red wine to the pan and bring to the boil. Peel the zest from the orange with a sharp knife or a vegetable parer and set aside. Squeeze the juice from the orange and add to the pan with a little seasoning. Lower the heat and cover tightly. Simmer for about 1 hour, until the duck is tender.

Meanwhile, cut the orange zest into thin slivers and blanch for a few seconds in a small pan of boiling water. Drain. Add the toasted pine nuts and brandy to the duck, stir gently and scatter the blanched orange zest on top. Cook for a further 10 minutes before serving.

CHICKEN ROASTED WITH LEMON AND OLIVES

In this recipe, chicken pieces are marinated in lemon juice, chilli and garlic, then roasted with the lemon halves and green olives. It relies on the natural sweetness of the lemons so do not use under-ripe fruit.

Serves 4

1.6 KG/3½ LB CORN-FED OR FREE-RANGE CHICKEN (OR 4 CHICKEN PORTIONS)

4 REALLY RIPE, JUICY LEMONS

8 GARLIC CLOVES

1 SMALL RED CHILLI, SEEDED AND SLICED INTO RINGS

15 ML/1 TBSP HONEY

175 G/6 OZ/1 CUP GREEN OLIVES

60 ML/4 TBSP CHOPPED FRESH PARSLEY

SALT AND FRESHLY GROUND BLACK PEPPER

Using a sharp knife and kitchen scissors, cut the chicken into 8 small or 4 large joints. Place in a shallow ovenproof baking dish. Squeeze the juice from the lemons and pour into a small bowl. Reserve the lemon halves. Peel 2 of the garlic cloves, crush them and stir into the lemon juice with the chilli and honey. Pour this mixture over the chicken and tuck the lemon halves around. Cover and leave to marinate for at least 2 hours, turning once or twice.

Turn the chicken skin-side up and place the lemon halves on top of it, cut-side down. Halve the remaining garlic cloves and scatter them over the chicken. Roast in an oven preheated to 200°C/400 °F/Gas Mark 6 for 45 minutes or until the chicken is golden brown and tender, adding the olives after 30 minutes. When the chicken is cooked, stir in the parsley, taste and season. Serve decorated with the roasted lemon halves.

VEGETABLES AND SALADS
INSALATA VERDE

Used as a showcase for Tuscan olive oil, this is the simplest of salads, often served as a course on its own in the middle of the meal as a kind of refresher for the palate. It could contain just one or two types of leaf – rocket is particularly fashionable these days and is often served by itself as a salad – but equally it might be a fanciful mix of many kinds of leaves and fresh herbs. Good leaves to choose from for flavour, texture and colour are rocket (arugula), curly endive, chicory (Belgian endive), treviso, radicchio, young spinach, and herbs such as parsley, basil, fennel, chives, etc. Balsamic vinegar can be used in the dressing and, with its aromatic sweetness, makes a good contrast to the quite bitter flavours of leaves such as radicchio, treviso and chicory. Choose a good-quality olive oil with a full, fruity and peppery taste to it.

Serves 4

ABOUT 125 G/4 OZ MIXED SALAD LEAVES, AS ABOVE

60 ML/4 TBSP EXTRA VIRGIN OLIVE OIL

COARSE SEA SALT

SPLASH OF BALSAMIC VINEGAR OR FRESHLY SQUEEZED LEMON JUICE

Wash the salad leaves and dry in a salad spinner. Pile into a salad bowl and toss lightly. Drizzle the oil over the salad and add the other seasonings. Toss again and serve at once.

ARTICHOKE AND BROAD BEAN (FAVA BEAN) STEW

A lovely vegetable stew made with small tender artichokes and, at best, early broad beans (fava beans) which are fresh and juicy. Frozen baby broad beans (fava beans) can be used if these are not available. Serve with focaccia or other bread.

Serves 4

6 SMALL, TENDER ARTICHOKES

1 LEMON, HALVED

60 ML/4 TBSP OLIVE OIL

300 G/10 OZ/1⅔ CUPS SHELLED BROAD BEANS (FAVA BEANS)

50 G/2 OZ/½ CUP PROVOLONE CHEESE, GRATED

150 ML/¼ PINT/⅔ CUP CHICKEN OR VEGETABLE STOCK

30 ML/2 TBSP TOMATO PURÉE

COARSE SALT AND FRESHLY GROUND BLACK PEPPER

CHOPPED FRESH PARSLEY, TO SERVE

Bring a pan of salted water to the boil. Pull off and discard the tough outer leaves of the artichokes. Cut them in half lengthwise and rub the cut surfaces with the lemon to prevent discoloration. Cook in the boiling water for 5 minutes, then drain thoroughly.

Heat about half the olive oil in a large saucepan. Add the broad beans (fava beans) and prepared artichokes, season and sprinkle the cheese on top. Spoon over the remaining olive oil. Stir together the hot stock and tomato purée and pour this into the pan. Bring to the boil, then lower the heat to barely simmering point, cover tightly and cook for 5 minutes. Serve hot, sprinkled with a little chopped parsley.

PANZANELLA (TUSCAN SALAD WITH ROASTED BREAD)

Day-old bread forms the foundation of a number of recipes in Tuscany, including Panzanella – a salad of bread, tomatoes, onions, basil and olive oil. In this version the bread is roasted first until golden and crisp and then added to the salad to soak up the dressing and juicy vegetable flavours. It makes a good starter or light lunch.

Serves 4

2 SWEET YELLOW PEPPERS

1 SWEET RED PEPPER

3 GARLIC CLOVES, UNPEELED

1 RED OR MILD ONION, PEELED AND THINLY SLICED

6 RIPE PLUM TOMATOES, CUT INTO WEDGES

HANDFUL OF BLACK OLIVES

HANDFUL OF FRESH BASIL LEAVES, ROUGHLY TORN

30 ML/2 TBSP CHOPPED FRESH PARSLEY

225 G/8 OZ FIRM-TEXTURED DAY-OLD COUNTRY BREAD, CUT INTO THICK SLICES, CRUSTS REMOVED

25 G/1 OZ/2 TBSP BUTTER, MELTED

SALT AND FRESHLY GROUND BLACK PEPPER

75 ML/5 TBSP EXTRA VIRGIN OLIVE OIL

JUICE OF ½ LEMON

15–30 ML/1–2 TBSP BALSAMIC VINEGAR

5 ML/1 TSP DIJON MUSTARD

Halve the peppers and remove the seeds. Place skin-side up on a grill rack (broiler rack) with the whole garlic cloves and cook under a hot grill (broiler) for 10–15 minutes, until the skins are blistered and blackened all over. Turn the garlic occasionally and push it to the edge of the grill (broiler) if it looks as if it might burn. Allow to cool slightly, then peel the peppers and cut the flesh into strips. Place in a large salad bowl. Set the garlic aside. Add the onion, tomatoes, olives and herbs to the salad bowl, season well and toss lightly to mix.

Brush the bread slices all over with the melted butter, then cut into large dice. Arrange in a single layer on a baking sheet and bake in an oven preheated to 200°C/400°F/Gas Mark 6 for 10–12 minutes, until crisp and a deep golden colour. Watch the bread carefully after 8 minutes as it tends to colour quickly after this.

Meanwhile, make the dressing: peel the grilled garlic and mash the flesh in a small bowl. Whisk in the olive oil, lemon juice, vinegar and mustard, then season to taste.

To serve, drizzle the dressing over the salad and toss well. Add the hot bread and toss again. Serve straight away.

ROASTED POTATOES WITH PANCETTA, GARLIC AND ROSEMARY

A delicious potato recipe! Serve hot as a vegetable dish or warm or cold as a salad – with or without the spicy, sweet-sharp flavouring of balsamic vinegar.

1 KG/2¼ LB SMALLISH NEW POTATOES, SCRUBBED

2 THICK SLICES OF SMOKED PANCETTA, ABOUT 125 G/4 OZ

75 ML/5 TBSP OLIVE OIL

3 GARLIC CLOVES, PEELED AND CRUSHED

30 ML/2 TBSP FRESH ROSEMARY 'SPIKES'

COARSE SEA SALT AND FRESHLY GROUND BLACK PEPPER

BALSAMIC VINEGAR, TO SERVE (OPTIONAL)

Cook the potatoes in a pan of boiling salted water for 10 minutes or until just tender, then drain. Roughly chop the pancetta and place in a shallow baking tin (baking pan) with the olive oil, garlic and rosemary. Add the potatoes and mix well to coat them thoroughly in the oil. Season and then roast in an oven preheated to 200°C/400°F/Gas Mark 6 for about 25 minutes, turning once or twice until golden. Serve splashed with a little balsamic vinegar, if liked.

GREEN BEANS WITH ONION, GARLIC AND CHILLI

Serves 4–6

45 ML/3 TBSP EXTRA VIRGIN OLIVE OIL

1 LARGE ONION, PEELED, HALVED AND SLICED

2 GARLIC CLOVES, PEELED AND CRUSHED

2.5–5 ML/½–1 TSP DRIED CHILLI FLAKES

1 LARGE RIPE TOMATO, SKINNED AND CHOPPED

450 G/1 LB GREEN BEANS, HALVED

SALT AND FRESHLY GROUND BLACK PEPPER

Heat the oil in a medium saucepan, add the onion and cook over a medium-high heat, stirring frequently, for 10 minutes, until tender and browned. Stir in the garlic and chilli flakes and continue cooking for 1 minute.

Add the tomato and beans to the pan with 150 ml/¼ pint/⅔ cup water. Season and bring to the boil, then lower the heat and cover the pan with a tight-fitting lid. Cook, stirring occasionally, for 15–20 minutes, until the beans are tender. Adjust the seasoning and serve hot or cold.

WHITE BEANS WITH TOMATO AND GARLIC SAUCE

One of Tuscany's most famous dishes, eaten as an accompaniment to all manner of meat courses, this has helped to earn the Tuscans their reputation throughout Italy as 'the bean eaters'.

Serves 4

450 G/1 LB/2¼ CUPS DRIED CANNELLINI BEANS

1 SMALL ONION, PEELED AND HALVED

2 CELERY STICKS

2 CARROTS, PEELED AND QUARTERED

SPRIG OF FRESH THYME

SPRIG OF FRESH SAGE PLUS 5 ML/1 TSP CHOPPED
   SAGE

4 GARLIC CLOVES, PEELED

SALT AND FRESHLY GROUND BLACK PEPPER

30 ML/2 TBSP OLIVE OIL, PLUS EXTRA FOR DRIZZLING

1 KG/2¼ LB LARGE RIPE TOMATOES, SKINNED, SEEDED
   AND CHOPPED

CHOPPED FRESH PARSLEY, TO GARNISH

Soak the beans overnight in water to cover. The next day, drain the beans, put them in a large saucepan and cover generously with fresh water. Add the onion, celery, carrots, herb sprigs and 2 of the garlic cloves, cut in half. Bring to the boil, then lower the heat, partially cover the pan with a lid and simmer for 1–1½ hours or until the beans are tender. Season with salt about 15 minutes before the end of the cooking time. Drain the beans, discarding the vegetables and herbs.

Crush the 2 remaining garlic cloves. Heat the oil in a large pan, add the garlic and the chopped sage and cook for 1 minute. Stir in the beans, tomatoes and some seasoning, then cook over a medium heat for about 20 minutes. Just before serving, drizzle the beans with olive oil and scatter with chopped parsley and a little more seasoning.

DESSERTS
ALMOND AND HAZELNUT BRITTLE

You can make brittle with almonds or hazelnuts or, as here, a mixture of the two. Serve as little sweetmeats with coffee or crush for sprinkling over ice cream or mascarpone.

Makes 700 g/ 1½ lb

325 G/11 OZ/2¾ CUPS BLANCHED HAZELNUTS
175 G/6 OZ/1½ CUPS BLANCHED ALMONDS
450 G/1 LB/2 CUPS CASTER SUGAR (SUPERFINE SUGAR)

60 ML/4 TBSP RUNNY HONEY (LIQUID HONEY)
5 ML/1 TSP FINELY GRATED LEMON ZEST
RICE PAPER
1 WHOLE LEMON, PREFERABLY UNWAXED

Spread the nuts on a baking sheet and toast in an oven preheated to 220°C/425°F/Gas Mark 7 for about 7 minutes, until lightly coloured.

Put the sugar and honey in a large, heavy-based saucepan and cook over a gentle heat for about 10 minutes, stirring until the sugar has dissolved. Leave to bubble over a moderately high heat until it is a rich brown colour. Remove from the heat and add the nuts and lemon zest. Stir over a very low heat until all the nuts are coated. Line a baking sheet with rice paper and turn the mixture on to this. Use the whole lemon to spread the brittle evenly, rolling it over the surface to form a slab about 2 cm/¾ inch thick – a lemon is ideal for this as the mixture doesn't stick to it and some of its flavour is imparted to the brittle. Cut the brittle into pieces with a large sharp knife while still warm or leave until set and shatter in a more random fashion. The brittle will keep in an airtight container for 1 month.

OVERLEAF: (FRONT LEFT) ALMOND AND HAZELNUT BRITTLE
(FRONT RIGHT) FRANGIPANE ICE CREAM (BACK) PANFORTE DI SIENA

PANFORTE DI SIENA

This flat, nougat-like cake is traditionally made in Siena from candied peel, honey, toasted nuts and spices. Serve it cut into thin wedges with a glass of sweet wine for dessert, or with coffee.

RICE PAPER

75 G/3 OZ/¾ CUP BLANCHED HAZELNUTS

75 G/3 OZ/¾ CUP BLANCHED ALMONDS

175 G/6 OZ/1 CUP CANDIED PEEL

75 G/3 OZ/¾ CUP PLAIN WHITE FLOUR (ALL-PURPOSE FLOUR)

2.5 ML/½ TSP GROUND CINNAMON

1.25 ML/¼ TSP FRESHLY GRATED NUTMEG

125 G/4 OZ/½ CUP CASTER SUGAR (SUPERFINE SUGAR)

125 G/4 OZ/½ CUP RUNNY HONEY (LIQUID HONEY)

ICING SUGAR (CONFECTIONERS' SUGAR) AND GROUND CINNAMON, FOR DUSTING

Line the base and sides of a 20-cm/8-inch loose-bottomed sandwich cake tin (round shallow cake pan) with rice paper. Spread the nuts on a baking sheet and toast in an oven preheated to 200°C/400°F/Gas Mark 6 for about 5 minutes, until golden. Leave to cool. Lower the oven temperature to 150°C/300°F/Gas Mark 2.

Chop the nuts roughly and place in a bowl with the candied peel, flour and spices. Mix well. Put the sugar and honey in a small pan and heat gently, stirring, until the sugar dissolves. Bring to boiling point and let it bubble for 5 minutes, then remove from the heat and pour on to the nut mixture. Stir until thoroughly combined, then turn the mixture into the prepared cake tin (cake pan) and spread flat (don't worry if it doesn't reach the top of the rice paper – you can trim this later). Bake in the oven for 30 minutes, until firm. Leave to cool slightly before removing from the tin (pan).

Before serving, tear off the excess rice paper around the top of the cake and dust liberally with a mixture of icing sugar (confectioners' sugar) and cinnamon.

CRISP, LIGHT BISCUITS WITH RICOTTA, COFFEE BEANS AND SUGAR

There couldn't be a better way to round off a meal than with these light, vanilla-flavoured biscuits for scooping up ricotta cheese sprinkled with coarsely ground coffee beans and crushed lump sugar. The biscuits are easy to make and could be flavoured with a little lemon or orange zest or almond extract instead of vanilla, if you wish. The best way to serve this dessert is to pile up the biscuits and let everyone help themselves to the ricotta and flavourings. Vin Santo or strong coffee make the perfect partners for it.

Makes 24 BISCUITS

125 G/4 OZ/½ CUP SOFTENED BUTTER
125 G/4 OZ/½ CUP CASTER SUGAR (SUPERFINE SUGAR)
150 G/5 OZ/1¼ CUPS PLAIN WHITE FLOUR (ALL-PURPOSE FLOUR)

2.5 ML/½ TSP BAKING POWDER
1 EGG YOLK
15 ML/1 TBSP DOUBLE CREAM (HEAVY CREAM)
2.5 ML/½ TSP NATURAL VANILLA EXTRACT

TO SERVE

RICOTTA CHEESE
COARSELY GROUND COFFEE BEANS

SUGAR, PREFERABLY CRUSHED LUMP SUGAR

To make the biscuits, beat all the ingredients together in a large bowl with a wooden spoon (or mix briefly in a food processor), blending evenly to give a smooth dough. Form into a short, fat roll about 5 cm/2 inches in diameter and wrap in baking parchment (wax paper) or cling film (plastic wrap). Chill for about 1 hour or until firm enough to slice. Line 2 baking sheets with baking parchment (wax paper). Cut the chilled dough into thin slices and place, well spaced apart, on the prepared baking sheets. Bake in an oven preheated to 190°C/375°F/Gas Mark 5 for about 10 minutes until firm and lightly coloured round the edges. As soon as the biscuits come out of the oven, lift them carefully off the baking sheets with a spatula and lay them over a rolling pin to curl as they cool. Transfer to a wire rack to cool completely. Serve with the ricotta, coffee and sugar, and with fresh fruit if liked.

NOTE

The biscuit mixture can be prepared in advance and kept in the fridge or freezer until ready for baking. Once baked, the biscuits will keep for a day or two in an airtight tin.

FRANGIPANE ICE CREAM

This is a simple vanilla ice cream containing chunks of baked almond frangipane. Serve with fruit or simply with crisp biscuits.

Serves 4 **ICE CREAM**	450 ml/¾ pint/2 cups full cream milk (whole milk)	6 egg yolks
	125 g/4 oz/½ cup caster sugar (superfine sugar)	7.5 ml/1½ tsp natural vanilla extract
		450 ml/¾ pint/2 cups double cream (heavy cream)
FRANGIPANE	75 g/3 oz/⅓ cup butter	1 egg yolk
	75 g/3 oz/⅓ cup caster sugar (superfine sugar)	1 tsp natural almond extract
	5 ml/1 tsp finely grated lemon zest	125 g/4 oz/1 cup ground almonds
	1 egg	25 g/1 oz/¼ cup plain white flour (all-purpose flour)

To make the ice cream, put the milk, sugar and egg yolks in a saucepan and beat together well. Heat gently, stirring, until the mixture thickens but take care not to let it boil or it will curdle. Strain into a large bowl, stir in the vanilla extract and leave to cool completely.

Lightly whip the cream and fold it into the cooled custard. Transfer to a freezerproof container, cover and freeze for about 1½ hours, until slushy.

Meanwhile, make the frangipane: grease and line the base of a 17.5-cm/7-inch sandwich cake tin (round shallow cake pan) with baking parchment (wax paper). Cream the butter, sugar and lemon zest together until light and fluffy. Gradually beat in the egg and yolk, followed by the almond extract. Fold in the ground almonds and flour. Spread the frangipane mixture in the prepared tin (pan) and bake in an oven preheated to 200°C/400°F/Gas Mark 6 for about 20 minutes, until set. Leave to cool completely in the tin, then turn out, peel off the paper and break the frangipane into small pieces.

Remove the partly frozen ice cream from the freezer and beat with a wooden spoon to help disperse ice crystals. Stir in the crumbled frangipane and refreeze until set. If time allows, stir the ice cream before it freezes solid. Remove from the freezer 20 minutes before serving.

RUSTIC STRAWBERRY TART

An almond tart sweetened with honey and topped with a strawberry glaze and fresh berries. Choose fresh ripe strawberries with lots of flavour or, if you can get them, scatter tiny wild strawberries on top. Serve with mascarpone.

Serves 6–8

PASTRY

175 G/6 OZ/1½ CUPS PLAIN WHITE FLOUR (ALL-PURPOSE FLOUR)

PINCH OF SALT

125 G/4 OZ/½ CUP BUTTER, CUT INTO SMALL PIECES

25 G/1 OZ/2 TBSP CASTER SUGAR (SUPERFINE SUGAR)

1 EGG, BEATEN

FILLING

200 G/7 OZ/1¾ CUPS GROUND ALMONDS

150 ML/¼ PINT/⅔ CUP SINGLE CREAM (LIGHT CREAM)

5 ML/1 TSP NATURAL ALMOND EXTRACT

45 ML/3 TBSP WELL-FLAVOURED RUNNY HONEY (LIQUID HONEY)

1 EGG

TOPPING

90 ML/6 TBSP STRAWBERRY JAM

45 ML/3 TBSP VIN SANTO OR OTHER DESSERT WINE

225 G/8 OZ/1½ CUPS RIPE STRAWBERRIES

A LITTLE ICING SUGAR (CONFECTIONERS' SUGAR), FOR DUSTING

To make the pastry, sift the flour and salt into a bowl. Rub in the butter using your fingertips, then stir in the sugar and egg and mix to a firm dough. Roll out on a floured board and use to line a 23-cm/9-inch buttered flan tin (tart pan). Chill for 20 minutes, then bake blind in an oven preheated to 200°C/400°F/Gas Mark 6 for 15 minutes, until lightly browned at the edges. Reduce the oven temperature to 180°C/350°F/Gas Mark 4.

Mix together all the filling ingredients and spread the mixture evenly in the pastry case. Bake in the oven for 20–25 minutes, until set.

Meanwhile, make the glaze: sieve the jam into a small pan, add the wine and heat gently. When the tart is cooked, pour the hot glaze over the top and then leave the tart to cool completely. Just before serving, scatter the strawberries over the top of the tart and dust with icing sugar (confectioners' sugar).

BOMBOLONI

These small, light, lemony doughnuts were a legacy left to the Tuscans by American soldiers demanding a taste of home during the Second World War.

25 G/1 OZ FRESH YEAST (COMPRESSED YEAST) OR 15 ML/1 TBSP DRIED ACTIVE YEAST

75 G/3 OZ/⅓ CUP CASTER SUGAR (SUPERFINE SUGAR)

75 G/3 OZ/⅓ CUP BUTTER

250 ML/8 FL OZ/1 CUP MILK OR WATER

450 G/1 LB/4 CUPS PLAIN WHITE FLOUR (ALL-PURPOSE FLOUR)

SALT

GRATED ZEST OF 1 LEMON

3 EGG YOLKS

2 EGG WHITES

OIL FOR DEEP-FRYING

EXTRA CASTER SUGAR (SUPERFINE SUGAR) OR VANILLA SUGAR, TO FINISH

Cream the yeast with 5 ml/1 tsp of the sugar. Melt the butter in a small saucepan, add the milk or water and heat to blood temperature. Meanwhile, sift the flour and salt into a bowl, stir in the remaining sugar and make a well in the centre. Pour the warm milk and butter on to the creamed yeast, mix well and pour into the well. Add the beaten egg yolks and lightly beaten whites, then mix by gradually drawing the flour in from the sides to form a smooth, light, sloppy dough. Beat this with your hand for 15 minutes, until smooth, glossy and elastic (or beat it in an electric mixer with a dough hook). Cover and leave to rise in a warm place for about 1½ hours or until doubled in size.

Turn out on to a well-floured work surface and knead until smooth. The dough will be quite soft. Flour a rolling pin well and roll out the dough to a thickness of 1.25 cm/½ inch. Stamp out rounds using a biscuit cutter (cookie cutter) or an upturned glass. Lay these on a well-floured cloth, cover with another·clean cloth and leave in a warm place to prove for about an hour, until puffed up.

Heat the oil to 180°C/350°F and fry the doughnuts in batches for about 6–8 minutes, until doubled in size and a deep golden brown. Lift out with a slotted spoon and drain on kitchen paper. Roll them in sugar while still warm, pile on to a plate and cover with a cloth to keep warm while you fry the remaining doughnuts. Serve warm.

BISCOTTI

Biscotti are hard biscuits, traditionally served with a glass of Vin Santo, a sweet dessert wine from Tuscany. The only way to eat them is to dip them in the wine to soften them and munch. They are very moreish. The name biscotti means twice-cooked. A very basic version of these biscuits was originally made for sailors to take on long voyages, as they kept well and did not go mouldy.

Makes about 50

175 G/6 OZ/1½ CUPS WHOLE BLANCHED ALMONDS, HAZELNUTS OR PINE NUTS

125 G/4 OZ/½ CUP SOFTENED UNSALTED BUTTER

200 G/7 OZ/1 SCANT CUP GRANULATED SUGAR

2 EGGS, BEATEN

FINELY GRATED ZEST OF 1 LEMON

15 ML/1 TBSP ANISEED LIQUEUR

7.5 ML/1½ TSP BAKING POWDER

2.5 ML/½ TSP SALT

ABOUT 350 G/12 OZ/3 CUPS PLAIN WHITE FLOUR (ALL-PURPOSE FLOUR)

75 G/3 OZ/¾ CUP COARSE POLENTA (CORNMEAL)

15 ML/1 TBSP FENNEL SEEDS OR ANISEED, LIGHTLY CRUSHED

Spread the almonds on a baking sheet and place in an oven preheated to 170°C/325°F/Gas Mark 3 for 5–10 minutes, until pale golden. Leave to cool, then coarsely chop a third of the nuts and mix them in with the remaining whole almonds.

Cream the butter with the sugar until just mixed, then beat in the eggs, lemon zest, liqueur, baking powder and salt. Stir in 275 g/10 oz/2½ cups of the flour, plus the polenta, almonds and crushed fennel seeds. Turn the dough on to a floured work surface and knead until smooth, adding the remaining flour little by little, if necessary, until the dough is soft but not sticky. Divide the dough into 4 and shape into long rolls 5 cm/2 inches wide and 1.5 cm/¾ inch thick. Place these on 2 greased baking sheets and bake for about 35 minutes, until just golden around the edges. Carefully transfer to a wire rack to cool for 10 minutes, then cut diagonally into slices 1.25 cm/½ inch thick. Place these cut-side down on the baking sheets and bake for another 10 minutes, until golden brown. Transfer to a wire rack to cool completely. Store in an airtight container for up to 1 week.

GRAPE BREAD

This rich, sweet flatbread made with fresh grapes and wine-soaked raisins comes from Florence. It may be served cold as a cake or warm as a pudding, with mascarpone cheese.

Serves 6–8

15 ML/1 TBSP ACTIVE DRY YEAST

1 TSP HONEY OR SUGAR

150 ML/¼ PINT/⅔ CUP LUKEWARM MILK

325 G/11 OZ/2¾ CUPS PLAIN WHITE FLOUR (ALL-PURPOSE FLOUR)

2.5 ML/½ TSP SALT

125 G/4 OZ/½ CUP CASTER SUGAR (SUPERFINE SUGAR)

1 EGG YOLK

175 G/6 OZ/1 CUP RAISINS

60 ML/4 TBSP VIN SANTO OR OTHER DESSERT WINE

450 G/1 LB SEEDLESS BLACK GRAPES

Put the yeast in a jug with the teaspoon of honey or sugar and the warm milk. Stir and leave to stand for 10 minutes, until frothy.

Sift the flour and salt into a bowl, make a well in the centre and add 75 g/3 oz/⅓ cup of the caster sugar (superfine sugar) and the egg yolk. Pour in the frothy yeast mixture and mix to form a fairly soft dough. Knead on a lightly floured surface for 5 minutes or until smooth and elastic, then place in a bowl and cover with a clean, damp cloth. Leave in a warm place to rise for about 40 minutes or until doubled in size. Meanwhile, soak the raisins in the Vin Santo and wash and dry the grapes.

Knock back the dough, knead again and divide in half. Shape into 2 rounds, each about 20 cm/8 inches in diameter. Place one on a large greased baking sheet and cover with half the raisins and grapes. Place the second round of dough on top and cover with the remaining fruit, pressing it lightly into the dough. Cover loosely and put to rise again for about 40 minutes or until doubled in size. Sprinkle the remaining sugar over the top and bake in an oven preheated to 190°C/375°F/Gas Mark 5 for about 45 minutes, until a deep golden colour. Serve warm or cold.

THE TUSCAN LARDER
SPICED PRESERVED PEARS

Fruits that have been picked when in their prime, poached in a sweet-sour sugar syrup and then preserved taste delicious, particularly when served with hot or cold ham. Do not use overripe fruit or it will discolour and disintegrate during cooking.

Makes about 900 g/2 lb

900 G/2 LB RIPE BUT FIRM UNBLEMISHED WILLIAMS PEARS
600 ML/1 PINT/2½ CUPS WHITE WINE VINEGAR
1 LEMON
450 G/1 LB/2 CUPS SUGAR

2.5 CM/1 INCH PIECE FRESH GINGER ROOT, THINLY SLICED
15 ML/1 TBSP ALLSPICE BERRIES
15 ML/1 TBSP CLOVES
1 LARGE CINNAMON STICK OR SEVERAL PIECES OF CASSIA BARK

Carefully peel the pears. Halve and quarter them and remove the cores. Place in a bowl of water with a dash of the vinegar in it to prevent discoloration. Pare the zest off the lemon in a single strip. Place the sugar and vinegar in a saucepan and heat gently to dissolve the sugar. When dissolved, add the ginger, lemon zest, spices and drained pears. Slowly bring to the boil and simmer gently for about 20 minutes or until the pears are tender – the pieces must remain whole. Lift out the pears with a slotted spoon and pack into sterilized preserving jars (canning jars), distributing the spices evenly. Bring the cooking liquid to the boil and boil for 10 minutes or until syrupy. Pour over the pears, making sure they are completely covered, and seal the jars. Store in a cool dark place for up to 6 months.

GRILLED PEPPERS AND CAPERS IN OIL

I like to make these with mostly red peppers, adding one or two yellow ones for colour. Serve as an antipasto, with grilled meat or fish, or with cheeses at the end of a meal. The peppers will keep happily in the fridge for a couple of weeks in a sterilized jar but should be brought to room temperature before serving.

5 MIXED-COLOUR (BELL) PEPPERS, HALVED AND SEEDED

60 ML/4 TBSP CAPERS IN VINEGAR, DRAINED

SMALL CAN OF ANCHOVY FILLETS, DRAINED

HANDFUL OF FRESH FLAT-LEAF PARSLEY

FEW SPRIGS OF FRESH OREGANO

FEW SPRIGS OF FRESH ROSEMARY

COARSELY GROUND BLACK PEPPER

EXTRA VIRGIN OLIVE OIL, TO COVER

Place the peppers skin-side up under a hot grill (broiler) and grill (broil) for 10–15 minutes, until well charred. Leave to cool slightly, then peel away the blackened skin and discard, along with the stalks. Cut the flesh of each half lengthwise into 3 pieces.

Meanwhile, rinse the capers and anchovy fillets, then pat dry on kitchen paper. Set aside about half the capers. Chop the rest with the anchovies, parsley and oregano to give a coarse paste. Take a tiny piece of the chopped caper mixture and place on one end of a pepper strip. Roll up and secure with a wooden cocktail stick. Continue with all the remaining mixture and peppers. Pack the rolled peppers into a sterilized preserving jar (canning jar) – or simply pile into a bowl if they are to be eaten within 2 days – with the rosemary sprigs, reserved capers and a generous grinding of black pepper. Pour over olive oil to cover. Store in the refrigerator.

CHAR-GRILLED AUBERGINES (EGGPLANT) PRESERVED IN OIL

Cook the aubergines (eggplant) on a cast-iron grill pan or over coals for a delicious smoky flavour.

2 AUBERGINES (EGGPLANT), CUT INTO SLICES ABOUT
1.25 CM/½ INCH THICK
10 ML/2 TSP SALT
15 ML/1 TBSP FENNEL SEEDS

4 SMALL SPRIGS OF FRESH ROSEMARY
LIGHT OLIVE OIL, FOR BRUSHING AND STORING
2 RED CHILLIES, HALVED AND SEEDED
2 GARLIC CLOVES, PEELED AND HALVED

Place the aubergine (eggplant) slices in a large colander and sprinkle with the salt. Leave to drain for 30 minutes, then rinse well and dry on kitchen paper.

In a small dry pan, heat the fennel seeds and rosemary for a few minutes to bring out their flavours. Set aside. Heat a cast-iron ridged grill pan until very hot. Liberally brush the aubergine (eggplant) slices on both sides with olive oil. Place them on the hot grill in batches and cook for 2–3 minutes on each side. Transfer to a plate. Add the chillies to the grill pan and cook for a couple of minutes at the end. Pack the prepared aubergines (eggplant) into a sterilized preserving jar (canning jar) with the fennel seeds, rosemary, chillies and garlic. Add sufficient olive oil to just cover and then seal. They will keep for 1 month. Serve with crusty bread and cheeses.

SWEET PEPPERS IN VINEGAR

Another method of preserving peppers, this time in vinegar. These should be made at least a couple of weeks ahead of using and will keep for up to 4 months.

4 LARGE RED AND/OR YELLOW (BELL) PEPPERS,
1 LITRE/1¾ PINTS/4 CUPS WHITE WINE VINEGAR
50 G/2 OZ/¼ CUP SUGAR

2.5 ML/½ TSP SALT
15 ML/1 TBSP BLACK PEPPERCORNS
2 SPRIGS OF FRESH BAY LEAVES

Cut the peppers lengthwise into quarters and remove the seeds and stalks. Put the vinegar, sugar, salt and peppercorns in a large saucepan and bring to the boil, stirring occasionally. Add the peppers and bring back to the boil, then lower the heat and simmer for 15 minutes. Add the whole sprigs of bay to the pan. Carefully transfer the peppers and bay to a sterilized preserving jar (canning jar) and then fill up with the hot vinegar. Seal the jar and leave for at least 2 weeks.

OVEN-ROASTED TOMATOES AND GARLIC IN OIL

Serve these with cheeses, salami and bread as antipasti or heat to make a simple sauce for pasta, adding a little cream and cheese, if liked. For exquisite flavour, use vibrant red tomatoes that have been ripened on the vine.

700 G/1½ LB RIPE CHERRY TOMATOES OR OTHER SMALL TOMATOES, HALVED

30 ML/2 TBSP CHOPPED FRESH THYME

4 SPRIGS OF FRESH OREGANO

75 ML/5 TBSP EXTRA VIRGIN OLIVE OIL, PLUS EXTRA TO COVER

2 HEADS OF GARLIC, DIVIDED INTO CLOVES AND PEELED

COARSE SALT AND FRESHLY GROUND BLACK PEPPER

Arrange the tomatoes cut-side up on one or two baking sheets. Sprinkle with the thyme and tuck the oregano sprigs among them. Drizzle over the olive oil and season with salt and pepper. Roast for 30 minutes in an oven preheated to 200°C/400°F/Gas Mark 6. Add the garlic cloves to the tomatoes, scattering them evenly, and return to the oven for a further 30–45 minutes, until the tomatoes are partially dried out and the garlic cloves are tender. Discard the sprigs of oregano.

Transfer the tomatoes and garlic to a sterilized preserving jar (canning jar) and pour over enough olive oil to cover. Serve cold or use in cooking. They will keep for 1 month.

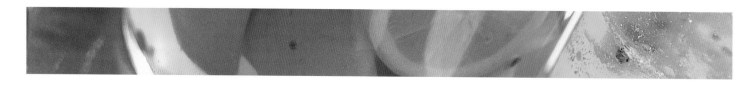

PRESERVED LEMONS

These lemons are particularly wonderful with chicken or fish dishes.

8 LEMONS

SEA SALT

5 ML/1 TSP BLACK PEPPERCORNS, CRUSHED

OLIVE OIL

3 GARLIC CLOVES, PEELED AND LIGHTLY CRUSHED

3 LARGE RED CHILLIES, SLIT OPEN

3 SPRIGS OF FRESH PARSLEY

HANDFUL OF GREEN OLIVES

VEGETABLE OIL

Cut the lemons in half and coat generously in sea salt. Set aside for 24 hours.

The next day, drain the lemons, then arrange them in layers in a sterilized preserving jar (canning jar), lightly sprinkling each layer with a little crushed pepper and some olive oil. Add a garlic clove, a chilli and a sprig of parsley to every third layer and arrange the olives in the middle. Cover the lemons with a combination of half olive oil and half vegetable oil, then seal and refrigerate for about 3 weeks before use.

HERBED OLIVES

A large bowl of these gleaming, aromatic, herby olives is perfect for serving with drinks for people to nibble.

BLACK OLIVES (NOT PITTED)

SPRIGS OF FRESH MARJORAM, ROSEMARY AND THYME

GARLIC CLOVES, PEELED AND THINLY SLICED

DRIED CHILLIES, TO TASTE (OPTIONAL)

Fill a sterilized preserving jar (canning jar) three quarters full with black olives. Add the herbs, garlic and chilli, if using – the quantities are entirely according to your preference. Fill up the jar with olive oil and seal tightly. Leave the olives to marinate in the oil for at least 2 weeks – the longer you leave them, the better the flavour. Use the olives within 6 months, then use the remaining oil in salad dressings.

INDEX